CONTENT

1 Social Interaction

KEY AIMS: By the end of Part 1 you will:
- ➤ understand how words and sentences work in social situations to influence other people;
- ➤ know about the role of non-verbal communication in social behaviour;
- ➤ see how verbal and non-verbal signals are linked.

The main topics to be dealt with in this Unit are *conformity*, *obedience* and *persuasion*, *leadership*, and *crowds*. However, all these processes are based on communication, and social interaction between people, so we will start with a brief account of communication and interaction.

Verbal communication

Some social encounters appear to consist entirely of speech, though as we shall see shortly, non-verbal communication takes place as well. Only in activities such as sports and dancing is there almost no speech. Look at a special kind of speech, when the umpire says 'Out', or the jury says 'Guilty', or Lady X declares this garden party open. These are called **performative utterances**, since they do something, they have an immediate effect on others – they are bits of social behaviour. All words uttered in social settings have this performative aspect, and we will regard utterances as pieces of social behaviour (Austin, 1962).

However, language is a special kind of social behaviour, in that it depends on words which have meanings, and syntax (the rules governing the grammatical

Figure 1.1: Social interaction.

1

arrangement of words) which enables us to combine words to make up messages. To communicate verbally we must have some words whose meanings are shared. This can be very simple, as with offering tea or coffee (vocabulary of two words), but by the age of six most children know the meanings of about 14,000 words. As people get to know each other better, or even as a conversation proceeds, their shared vocabulary increases, for example, during a school lesson. Often utterances add new shared information to what is already there, as in 'The coffee machine has conked out again'.

In order to send a verbal message to someone else it is necessary to put it in a form which they will understand and which is likely to have the desired effect on them. It is necessary to 'take the role of the other', sometimes known as **intersubjectivity**. Most people do this most of the time; for example, they will speak differently to a child than to a dog; mechanics speak differently to customers than to other garage people (the former may not know the difference between a carburettor and a spark plug), and lawyers speak differently to other lawyers.

If you want to have some kind of social influence, the message must be designed in a skilled way; utterances need to be polite and persuasive if they are going to work. For example, 'Post this letter' might not have the desired effect, but 'If you're passing the letter box, would you mind posting this?' might get the letter posted.

Making up sentences also requires some competence at grammar. A sentence without a verb, or which breaks the rules in other ways, may convey no meaning. However, people may communicate perfectly well while breaking the normal grammatical rules; for example, 'I don't bother nobody', the double negative common in 'Black English Vernacular'.

SAQ 1

Why is it important to think about the other person's point of view when speaking to them?

Different kinds of utterance

There are three basic kinds of utterance which play central roles in social behaviour:

1   *Orders and instructions*. Here words are used to influence others, and may take the form of orders, instructions or persuasion. We shall see later that all kinds of social influence involve such utterances, and that the success of persuasion and leadership depends on the skilful construction of these communications.

2   *Questions*. These are a special kind of order, intended to obtain information. Questions can be open-ended or closed; for example, an open-ended question would be, 'What did you do this summer?', requiring a detailed answer, while an example of a closed question would be, 'Did you go abroad this summer?', requiring only a 'yes' or 'no' answer.

3   *Information*. This was probably important in the evolution of language – telling others about things not immediately present, such as animals, food and water. Information can be given in reply to a question, as part of a lecture, or in discussion.

There are several other common kinds of utterance:

4   *Performative utterances*. We gave some examples earlier; others would be voting, promising, and making a bet. In all these cases the utterances are not true or false, they are social acts.

5   *Informal speech*. This includes chat, jokes, and gossip. Little useful information may be conveyed, but the purpose is more to strengthen and enjoy social relationships.

6   *Expression of emotions and attitudes to others*. This can be important, as in 'I love you', but these matters are normally expressed non-verbally, and that channel is generally more effective. We find that non-verbal style has much more effect than the words used – 'actions speak louder than words' – and the particular actions here are tone of voice, facial expression and so on.

7   *Social routines*. These include greeting, thanking, and apologizing. They are of interest since they have a standard, ritual, form to them, especially in the case of greeting.

8   *Latent messages*. This is where the real purpose of the utterance is concealed, as in 'As I was saying to the Prime Minister' – though the real purpose is too obvious in this case.

Conversation

Most social behaviour involves conversation; that is, a sequence of utterances. Persuasion usually needs more than one utterance to do the job, for example. Some individuals find it very difficult to sustain a conversation, so what is it that they need to know which would help them? There seem to be rules about how utterances are put together in order to make up a conversation; there is a kind of 'grammar' of conversations. So what is it?

To begin with, conversations are constructed out of smaller building blocks, consisting of pairs of utterances which go together. The most common pair is question–answer, where the answer is closely related to the question, and is meaningless without it; for example, 'ninety miles' is useless unless we know that the question was 'How far is Oxford from Cambridge?'. There are variations on this theme; for example, an 'open-ended' question, such as 'What did you do in the holidays?' will lead to a longer answer than a closed one like 'Did you go to Spain?'.

There are longer sequences than this. According to the *motor skill model* of social behaviour, interactors are trying to elicit some kind of response from one another, and if the first approach fails they respond to this by modifying their approach and trying again. *Figure* 1.2 shows this schematically.

This leads to sequences of at least four steps, as for example in a social survey interview:

Interviewer: *asks question*.
Respondent: *gives useless answer, or doesn't understand question*.
Interviewer: *clarifies and repeats question*.
Respondent: *gives useful answer*.

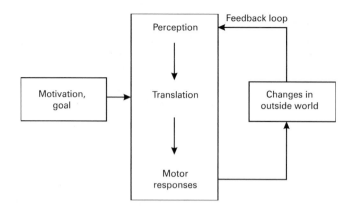

Figure 1.2: Motor skills model (from Argyle, 1994).

Sometimes there are repeated cycles of behaviour. This can happen in the school classroom, as shown in *Figure* 1.3.

The lesson may start with a repeated cycle of questions and answers such as, 'What is the capital of France?' – 'Paris', and so on. There may be a longer cycle of lecture–question–answer, or a longer one still where pupils are encouraged to initiate ideas. Note that the teacher's questions are very odd since he or she probably knows the answers already. He or she is also making a double, or 'pro-active', move, lecturing and then asking a question, apparently responding to him or herself. Note that what has been described is actually a cycle of cycles.

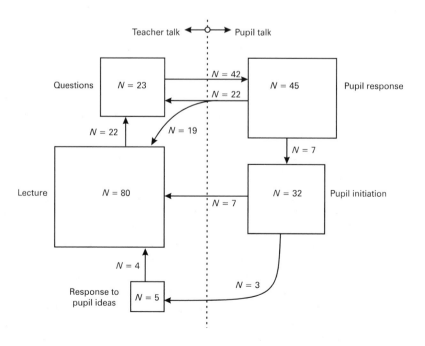

Figure 1.3: Cycles of interaction in the classroom (Flanders, 1970).

Accommodation

People speak in very different ways, in different languages and accents, at different speeds, and at different levels of loudness. When two people converse they often converge to similar styles, partly to be able to make themselves understood, but partly to be accepted more by the other. Individuals will usually **accommodate** more to the other if they are very keen to be approved of, and if they are in a position of less power or status than the other.

This topic was investigated by Giles and Coupland (1991), working in Bristol, UK. Coupland investigated the dropping of h's (for example, saying 'otel' instead of 'hotel') by a girl in a travel agency. It was found that her rate of h-dropping varied between 3.7 per cent and 29.3 per cent depending on the h-dropping rate of the client she was talking to, and her rate correlated highly with that of clients.

Accommodation is found to work, in that if the other converges to the same style as the speaker they are liked more. So convergence is part of the skill of verbal communication.

Politeness

This is not a joke topic about taking hats off to ladies, but a serious aspect of verbal skills. It is about avoiding offence and avoiding damaging another's self-esteem. Politeness could be defined as 'forms of speech which are as far as possible agreeable and rewarding to others'; only 'as far as possible', because sometimes we need to disagree or fail to comply with others' wishes.

There are several aspects of politeness: care of the other person's self-esteem, for example, praising them rather than yourself, avoiding constraining them, giving them a choice, being careful how disagreement is expressed.

Politeness is a serious matter. In a study of aircrews it was found that when crews were polite to the pilot, there were fewer accidents; but if there was an emergency politeness was no good – 'I'm sorry to bother you, Captain, while you are having your coffee, but have you noticed that the port wing is on fire?'. More effective would be 'Bloody wing's on fire' (Linde, 1988).

In Japan and Hong Kong however, the rules of politeness are much more demanding because of the great concern over possible loss of face. In addition to not saying 'No', it is not as acceptable to joke or tease friends as it is in Britain (Argyle, 1987).

 SOMETHING TO TRY

1. Ask two people to role-play a meal where one wants the salt, while varying the social status of the second. What does the first person say? The prediction is that there will be more indirectness, disguising the request as a question, and offering choice, when the person being asked to pass the salt is of higher status.
2. Arrange a conversation between two people where one is more technically informed on a subject than the other. How far does the expert take the role of the other and try to make him or herself easily understood?
3. Try to give examples of an effective way and a non-effective way of asking a favour of some kind.

SAQ
2

Why is politeness important? What is usually meant by politeness?

Non-Verbal Communication (NVC)

Social interaction doesn't consist only of words; there are also the signals of facial expression, tone of voice, and gestures which make up **non-verbal communication**. For example, when we discuss experiments on obedience later, the very dominant tone of voice used by the experimenter is a crucial part of the story. When we discuss leadership, we shall see that it is necessary to convey friendly and dominant attitudes at the same time. We shall see that persuasion is more successful if the source of influence is seen as more likeable or expert, and these qualities are mainly conveyed non-verbally.

Non-verbal signals do several jobs: they express emotions and attitudes to others, such as whether we like them or not, and they have more impact than words in both of these spheres. They play an important part in supporting and adding to speech and they are the main method of **self-presentation**; that is, telling other people about ourselves.

Most non-verbal signals are encoded by the sender from some inner state, for example, anger into a frown, and are then decoded by the recipient, as in *Figure* 1.4.

Figure 1.4: Encoding and decoding non-verbal signals (Argyle, 1994).

Sometimes the sender is unaware of the message he or she is sending, though it may be perfectly clear to the receiver. Sometimes neither is aware of it, as in the dilation of the pupils of the eyes in sexual attraction which affects the receiver though he or she doesn't know how.

Some research has been done on encoding; for example, putting participants into some emotional state by showing them suitable videos which will make them happy or sad, and seeing what facial expressions they have, or putting them with people they like for the same purpose. Other research done on decoding has involved showing specially prepared films, or playing tapes to see how participants interpret them.

The different functions of NVC

Expressing emotions
The face is the most effective channel for expressing emotion, but the voice and the body are better for decoding emotions which are being concealed –

they are both 'leakier' than the face. Ekman and Friesen (1969) found that judges who saw videotapes of target persons in different emotional states, and who could only see the body, made more accurate ratings of negative emotions than those who saw the face.

Expressing interpersonal attitudes

The main signals indicating liking for another person are:

- smile
- gaze
- proximity, side-by-side orientation (except while eating)
- touch
- open arm posture (not folded or on hips)
- voice of raised pitch, rising pitch and pure tone.

We have found that such non-verbal signals created a much stronger impression of liking than equated verbal messages.

On the other hand, dominance is conveyed by:

- non-smiling, frowning face
- posture: full height, expanded chest, hands on hips
- occupation of a high status area, for example, behind a desk
- gestures – pointing at the other person or their property
- touching, but not being touched back
- gaze, but mainly while talking, less while the other is talking
- voice: loud, slow, interrupting, a lot of talk

However, a more relaxed style is used if status has already been established.

Supporting verbal communication

A lot of non-verbal communication is used to accompany and support speech. The person speaking uses a lot of variations in pitch and emphasis, to 'frame' what he or she is saying, as funny, serious, sarcastic, trivial and so on. They may also use a lot of illustrative gestures to add to their words, and they look at the other person at the end of long sentences and at the end of the utterance – these are the points at which they need feedback.

Meanwhile the listener provides feedback by his or her facial expression, some head-nods or shakes, and posture. They may vocalize, especially over the telephone, with 'Really?', 'How nice', and so on, or may complete the sentence for the speaker.

When two people are talking, they achieve a high level of synchrony, in that as soon as one stops speaking the other usually begins, without pauses or interruption. How is this done? The first cue to be discovered was the 'terminal gaze', given as speakers are about to stop, and shown in *Figure* 1.5.

In this study it was found that if a speaker failed to give a terminal gaze there was a pause before the other replied, so the gaze evidently functions as a full-stop signal. There are other cues – for example, the falling pitch as a sentence ends, unless it is a question, in which case it rises. The listener can anticipate

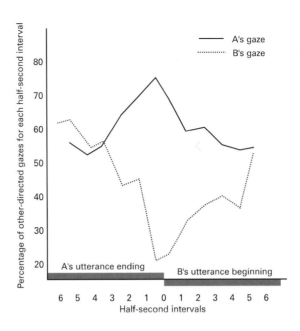

Figure 1.5: The timing of looks in relation to speech (Kendon, 1967).

the end of a sentence from its verbal structure, and as speakers stop speaking, they put their hands to rest and stop gesturing.

The different non-verbal channels

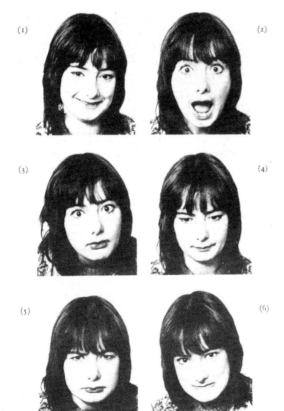

Facial expression

This is the most important non-verbal channel. For expressing emotions, six main facial expressions have been found, as shown in *Figure* 1.6.

These six kinds of facial expressions are found in all cultures, and something similar is found in monkeys. They are controlled by the facial nerves, and are partly innate. However, since we are still able to smile when feeling cross, for example, there is clearly a second process, and there is a second facial nerve from higher in the brain, an area which is more affected by past learning and more under voluntary control, which can over-ride the one from the mid-brain.

Figure 1.6: The six main facial expressions: (1) happiness; (2) surprise; (3) fear; (4) sadness; (5) anger; (6) disgust.

Ekman and Friesen (1969) showed a film of a sinus operation to American and Japanese participants, who were alone but were secretly filmed. Both groups of participants showed a 'disgust face' while watching the film, but when interviewed about it the Japanese smiled. There are 'display rules' in Japan which discourage making nasty faces in public. When watching TV alone people do make facial expressions, though these are much weaker than those made when others are present.

People tend to exercise a lot of control over their facial expressions. Quite young children know that it is best to pretend to be pleased when given a present they don't like, and to show facial expressions which will avoid trouble. But this control doesn't always succeed, and there can be 'leakage' of the true emotion or attitude. A nervous public speaker or interviewee may perspire, clench their hands or have a shaky voice.

Tone of voice

Tone of voice can indicate emotions and attitudes to others just as the face can. Scherer (1981) generated nearly two hundred sounds from an electronic music machine and asked people to decode the emotions conveyed by the machine. The results were clear: depression, for example, was conveyed by a sound which was slow, with a low and falling pitch. Anger was conveyed by a loud and discordant voice, happiness by a raised pitch, with gentle and upward pitch changes, and pure tone.

Another way of studying tones of voice is to ask one person (the sender) to read the paper or lists of numbers in different emotional styles, and see if the listener (the receiver) can decode them correctly. There are big individual differences in ability both to send and to receive.

Tone of voice is nearly as good as facial expression for communicating emotions, but there is an interesting difference – the voice is 'leakier'; that is, it fails to conceal true feelings as well as the face does. So if you want to know what someone else is really feeling, attend to their voice rather than their face. This is what men tend to do, while women have been described as 'polite decoders' since they watch the face and receive what the sender wants them to receive. The explanation of all this is probably that the female sub-culture is more co-operative and trusting than the competitive and deceptive male sub-culture (Rosenthal and DePaulo, 1979).

Other non-verbal signals

As we saw earlier, emotions and attitudes to others are expressed by a number of non-verbal signals. Emotions and attitudes to others also use *posture, bodily contact* and *spatial behaviour*. Speech is supported by *gestures, tone of voice* and *shifts of gaze*. **Self-presentation** is mainly managed by appearance, and by tone of voice.

 SOMETHING TO TRY

1. *Watch several pairs of individuals from a window, where you can see them but not hear them. What do you think the relationship between them is? What non-verbal signals did you use to decide?*
2. *Choose one or more individuals from a different cultural background to your own. Are there ways in which their non-verbal signals differ to those of your culture?*

Can you think of some clues we can look for to help us find out what other people are really feeling?

Why do we humans make so much use of NVC? Why does it have such a powerful effect?

Conformity

KEY AIMS: By the end of Part 2 you will be able to:
➢ *find out the conditions under which people conform;*
➢ *understand the processes involved;*
➢ *see how minorities may influence groups;*
➢ *see when people form and follow rules, and when they break them.*

It seems to be a universal law of social groups that they form norms. A **norm** is a pattern of behaviour, beliefs or attitudes which is shared by most members of a group. If members deviate they may be put under social pressure to conform, and usually do so. However, some do not, and they may be rejected, or they may be able to change the norm.

At one time it was common for there to be output restriction norms among factory workers to prevent workers working too fast – it was feared that rates of pay might be reduced to prevent workers from earning too much. Norms about clothes are found in all groups, and teenagers seem particularly keen to conform to such norms. However, it is also necessary to be *different* from others, but still within the norms! There are norms about beliefs in religious and political groups; for example, a church member who denies key beliefs will be very unpopular.

Norms develop on matters which are important to the group. They are very useful, since they embody patterns of behaviour which have been found to work in the past and they also produce similar behaviour in group members, which can be very useful in a working group for example. On the other hand, deviates are useful too, since they may introduce new ideas, and prevent the group from becoming out of date.

Social psychologists have carried out many ingenious experiments to find out how norms work, who conforms, who deviates, and so on.

Classic laboratory experiments

One of the earliest experiments in social psychology was Sherif's study (1935) of the formation of a social norm. He used the **autokinetic effect** – when a spot of light seen in the dark seems to move. Sherif put groups of three participants in a dark room, a point of light was shone 15 feet away from them for several seconds, and participants were asked to say how far it moved. Estimates of two to eight inches were given. This was repeated on three further days, and it was found that judgements converged. An example of Sherif's data is shown in *Figure* 2.1.

This is a neat demonstration of a norm developing, but it is a very unusual case since there is no objective reality here – the light does not move and the apparent movement is an illusion.

In the experiments by Asch (1956), on the other hand, a real stimulus was used – the lengths of different lines on a card. Participants were shown pairs of cards like those in *Figure* 2.2, placed 40 inches apart.

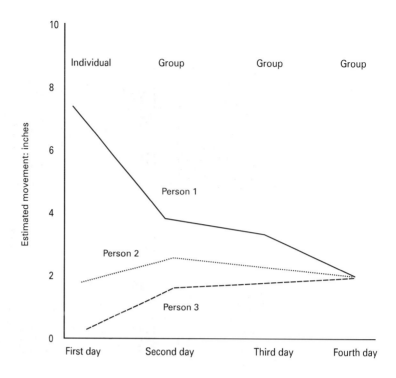

Figure 2.1: A sample group form Sherif's study of norm formation. Three individuals converge as they give repeated estimates of the apparent movement of a point of light. (Data from Sherif and Sherif, 1969, redrawn by Myers, 1993.)

The task was to say which of the lines on the right, A, B, or C, was the same length as the one on the left. However, the participants found that they were one of a group of seven or eight, and on certain crucial trials were the last one to give their judgement when all the others had given the wrong answer, because they were confederates of the experimenter. *Figure* 2.3 shows a participant looking worried while trying to decide what to say. Overall, a third of the responses on crucial trials were wrong, that is, they agreed with the majority, and two thirds were correct. About a quarter of the participants never conformed, and about a quarter nearly always did.

Asch also interviewed the participants afterwards and asked them why they had given the wrong answers. Some said that they did it in order not look silly or be rejected by the rest of the group. Others said it was because the others must have better eyesight or be better informed in some way; in other words, they used the judgements of the others as a source of information.

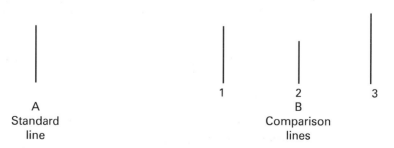

Figure 2.2: An example of the stimuli presented in Asch's experiment (Asch, 1956).

Figure 2.3: Conformity pressures in the Asch experiment (from Myers, 1993).

Is it any good asking people to explain this kind of behaviour, or is it due to automatic processes which are hard to explain, like staying upright on a bicycle?

Another experimental procedure was devised by Schachter (1951). Groups were given the task of deciding the best solution to a human relations problem, such as how to deal with a problem child. In each group there was one (female) confederate, who consistently deviated; the others first tried to influence her, and then gave up and ignored her – she was rejected. This is one possible law of social behaviour: 'deviation leads to rejection'.

Why do people conform?

We have just had a preview of the answer in Asch's interviews: people **conform** either in order not to be rejected, or because they think the group knows better than they do themselves. These are usually called the 'normative' and 'informational' kinds of influence. **Normative influence** is greater if judgements have to be made in public rather than in private – there is much more conformity for public judgements, and also when there is competition between groups to produce fewest errors, or to be co-operative. **Informational influence** is greater if the other members are more expert or informed, or if participants are made to believe that they are, and if the task is difficult.

SAQ

4

Why do people conform to norms?

The most interesting case is the difference between public and private. Sometimes individuals are under great pressure to do or say things which they do not believe in, for example in racial or military situations – perhaps if they don't shoot someone they will be shot themselves, or if they back a minority group member they will themselves be fired. If they conform in these cases it is **compliance**, but there is no **internalization**, since they don't believe in what they are doing. They would not do it when away from the group, and they would not want to persuade other members of the group to conform. On the other hand, when an individual has conformed in this way they sometimes start to look at things differently, so that their conformity is justified (Buehler and Griffin, 1994). This is a rediscovery of an older principle, that if people are coerced into doing or saying something that they don't believe in, it produces a state of conflict or 'dissonance'. One way of reducing this is to change private beliefs to be consistent with behaviour, for example, after going to church under social pressure.

If a individual in a conformity experiment is given a companion, who is also a **naïve participant** in the experiment, this person is seen as a supporter, and the amount of conformity is much reduced. But is this due to normative or to informational influence? Probably both. Allen and Levine (1971) studied the effects of different kinds of supporters; they all reduced conformity on the part of the individual supported, even if the supporter had such bad eyesight that he couldn't be a source of valid information. So it seems that this support was mainly normative.

SAQ
5

What is the main difference between compliance and conformity?

Conformity in religious cults

There have been a number of incidents recently in which the members of religious cults have committed mass suicide. There seems to be a very high degree of conformity, together with obedience, in these cults. In a milder incident, in 1951, the members of a small end-of-the world cult gathered on a hilltop in Minnesota waiting to be rescued by flying saucers. When this did not happen the leader worked out a revised date, and efforts were made to recruit new members. When the world did not end the second time the cult broke up. The interpretation of this sequence of events may be that when physical reality failed to support the members' beliefs, they needed more 'social reality' to replace it, in the form of more believing members (Festinger *et al.*, 1956). Religious groups in general are rather short of *physical* reality, which may be why some groups are intolerant of unbelievers, or those whose faith is thought to be 'unsound'. This is most true of fundamentalist churches; liberal ones tend to be more tolerant. There is certainly a lot of social support in general in churches; many members say that their closest friends belong to their church (Beit-Hallahmi and Argyle, 1997).

When do people conform most?

We have discussed some of the variables already; for example, people conform when their behaviour is publicly visible to the rest of the group, and they conform more if the group is larger and if all the others agree. At least, it seems

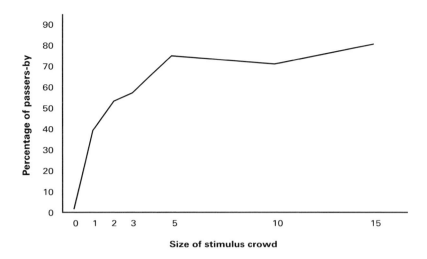

Figure 2.4: Group size and conformity. The percentage of passers-by who imitated a group looking upward increased as group size increased to five persons. (From Myers, 1993.)

to make a difference in groups of up to about five or six members in the kind of experiment we have been discussing. *Figure* 2.4 is from a study by Milgram *et al.* (1969) who arranged for groups of different numbers of confederates to stand and look upwards in the street to see how many passers-by would do the same.

In the Asch-type experiments, adding more stooges increased conformity only if they were seen as individuals who were making up their own minds, not just following each other, nor a group which had worked out the answers already. We saw earlier that there was more conformity when there was unanimity in the rest of the group, and less when there were other deviates, whether they acted as supporters or not.

Individuals conform a lot more to the norms of groups whose members they like, and to which they want to belong. Crandall (1988) found that there was conformity among female students in tendencies to binge eating – they did the same as their friends. In an early classic study, Newcomb (1943) found that students conformed to the political norm of the group that they wanted to be accepted by – either the left-wing college community or their right-wing home community in this case. There is likely to be internalization too, through identification with, and imitation of, the admired members of such groups.

There is more conformity when the norm is *directive*; that is, says what ought to be done, indicates what is approved or disapproved of, rather than just *descriptive* – saying that this is what most people do. This was shown in an ingenious experiment about litter norms where handbills were placed on cars in a car park. It was found that these were thrown away less often if the parking lot was very tidy (*descriptive norm*), and people were much tidier if a confederate was seen to be picking litter up (indicating *disapproval*) (Reno *et al.*, 1993).

SAQ
6

List three conditions when you would expect most conformity in a group.

Gender

Do women conform more than men? In some of the early experiments they did appear to conform more, though the difference was small, but more recent studies have not found this. It is widely believed that women conform more and are more easily influenced, perhaps because women often have lower status positions, and individuals of lower status are more easily influenced; we shall see examples of this when we discuss obedience. Eagly and Wood (1982) gave participants in their study little stories in which one employee was trying to influence another. If no information was given about the status of the two people, they found that it was more frequently thought that a male would be able to influence a female, but if information about job status was given, it was the person of lower status who was influenced more, and gender had no effect.

Personality

Is there a kind of conformist personality? There has been much research on the topic, but the relationship with familiar personality traits is very weak – situational factors are more important. This is partly because experiments on conformity have used very strong social pressures – personality might emerge more clearly if milder situations were used.

One personality trait which has had some success here is **self-monitoring**. High self-monitors are individuals who are keen to be accepted in every situation, and who monitor and control their own behaviour accordingly. Low self-monitors, on the other hand, like to be genuine and sincere and present themselves as they really are. There are many interesting findings about this personality variable, but the key one for us is that high self-monitors conform more, in public that is, while low self-monitors carry on displaying their true opinions regardless of whether or not others like them (Snyder, 1979).

Another interesting personality variable is the *desire for uniqueness*. We all want to be unique, in the right way, and preferably better than other, 'ordinary', people. This desire can be aroused experimentally: if people are told that the attitudes which they have just expressed are nearly the same as those of thousands of other students, they are found to conform less in the next experiment. Some people feel unique anyway, for example if they have red hair, or come from a minority group; it is likely that they will conform less too (Snyder and Fromkin, 1990).

Culture

The Asch experiment has been replicated in different cultures more than any other social psychology experiment. In the original study in 1956, 37 per cent conformed, but the average for the eight American studies carried out since then was 25 per cent. In **collectivist cultures** the percentages are higher than this; for example, Zimbabwe 51 per cent, India 58 per cent, and there have been high values in other Asian countries. In these cultures the group is very important and harmony must be maintained. In America and Europe the percentages of people conforming were lower – the average of four British studies was 17 per cent while the average of two Belgian studies was 19 per cent. In these cultures individual responsibility is valued. If recent studies are compared with those of 40 years ago, it can be noted that the level of conformity has fallen in Europe and the USA.

These replications have shown something else. There is more conformity in intact groups; that is, within groups of people who know each other, or think they have something in common, like sports teams. There is more conformity in groups of students than in groups of adult strangers, and there was 39 per cent conformity for unemployed British black people. It seems that there is more conformity where is a feeling of interdependence on each other (Smith and Bond, 1993).

SAQ
7

Which affects the degree of a person's conformity most – gender, personality or culture?

The effect of minorities

American research in this area has tended to concentrate on conformity, but European research has been more interested in how changes in groups are brought about by minorities. This all started with an experiment by Serge Moscovici and colleagues in Paris, a kind of Asch experiment in reverse, with groups made up of two confederates and four 'real' participants. The task was to say whether each of 36 slides shown to them was green or blue. All were clearly blue, but they differed in intensity. In one condition, the 'consistent' condition, the confederates always said 'green'; in the 'inconsistent' condition they said 'green' 24 times and 'blue' 12 times; and in the control condition there were groups of naïve participants. With the consistent minority, 8.4 per cent of participants were influenced, with the inconsistent minority 1.25 per cent were influenced, and for the controls only 0.25 per cent thought the slides were green (see *Figure* 2.5).

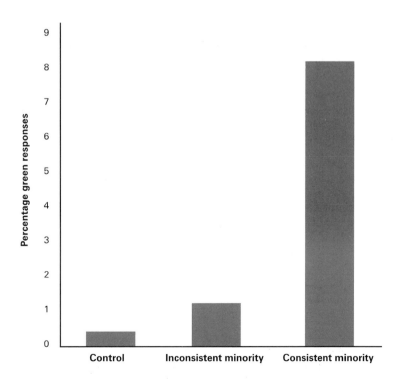

Figure 2.5: Percentage of green responses given by the majority group participants in the experiment by Moscovici, Lage and Naffrechoux (1969).

This experiment could be criticized on the grounds that judging colours is far removed from most everyday conformity, or that the experimental conditions are complex and confusing. However, this study has led to a considerable body of later research which has produced consistent and very interesting findings.

In one of them, Nemeth and others (1974) did a similar experiment, but now the confederates could say either 'green' or 'green–blue' – all the slides still being blue. If they gave these two alternatives at random there was no effect on the majority, but if they gave them in a consistent way, green to the brighter slides, and green-blue to the dimmer ones, there was an amazing 21 per cent influence. This suggests that flexibility may be important as well as consistency, and several experiments have found that there is more minority influence if the minority behave in a flexible way, and are willing to negotiate and compromise.

How do minorities have this power to change the majority? They have less power to exert normative influence, so perhaps they exert informational influence of some kind. A consistent minority has to be taken seriously, especially when they hold firm under social pressure; the majority view may start to be questioned and other solutions considered, so group members start thinking. This was Moscovici's view – that minorities may affect how people think, while majorities affect their behaviour and may produce compliance but not necessarily conversion.

This was supported in an experiment in which pairs of subjects were shown five blue slides. One of the pair was a confederate who always said the slides were green, and the real subjects were told that this was the judgement of either the majority or the minority of other subjects. In a later trial, subjects were asked to write down the colour of the slide and the colour of its **after-image**, seen on a blank wall (this is the 'opposite' of the colour just seen). More of the subjects who had been told that the minority thought the slides were green saw the after-image of green, that is, red-purple, rather than that of blue, which is yellow-orange: if they were told that the minority saw it as green they saw green. Telling them that the majority saw the slides were green had a smaller effect (Moscovici and Personnaz, 1980).

Later work has not confirmed the idea that majority and minority influences are quite different. It seems that both forms of influence can affect both private and public responses, but there is still evidence that minority influence sets off more thoughtful reactions, and may stimulate more original solutions to problems. Minorities may play an important role in society. Whether or not people like them, they are an important source of social change (van Avermaet, 1995).

SAQ
8

Which factors are important in determining when a minority is most likely to be able to influence the majority?

Social rules

Social rules are like norms in many ways, but are different. Take the rule of the road – keep to the left. This is not a matter of degree, it must be followed, as it doesn't just lead to disapproval but to total chaos if it is disobeyed. And it was devised to solve a social problem, that of avoiding head-on collisions.

In this case there are at least two ways of solving the problem – keep to the left or to the right. The difference between rules and norms can be seen in cricket – if you wear the wrong coloured trousers it may annoy people, but if you use a tennis racket the game will stop. The rules of games do more than solve problems, they make a whole new sphere of activity possible.

In a companion unit in this series, *Social Relationships* (Argyle, 1998), the rules of different relationships are described; these too solve problems. So for next-door-neighbours we find rules such as 'Be considerate about noise, pets, children and activities', and 'Don't encroach over shared boundaries'. We also report on the surprising degree of rule-following in apparently disorderly situations, such as fighting between women and between rival groups of football hooligans.

The study of rules has also shed light on why some people break them, and these findings apply equally to norms. We asked people to describe instances of rule-breaking, by themselves or others, which they had seen, and to offer the likely reasons for it. Some of these reasons are familiar and obvious, others less so. They include:

- anti-social short-cuts, such as pushing into a queue
- ignorance of the rules, for example, by a newcomer
- trying to be funny, perhaps wearing fancy dress
- attempt to improve procedures, for example, picking up a football and inventing rugby
- incompetence due to drink or forgetfulness
- situational pressures, due to conflict of rules, or apparent crisis.

Another reason has now been found: people sometimes deviate because they are conforming to the norms of another group, to which they have belonged in the past or currently belong to.

SAQ
9

Why does breaking a rule cause so much trouble?

SOMETHING TO TRY

Investigate a social group, and try to find what appear to be some of its norms or rules. This can be done by asking members of the group what things are particularly disapproved of in this group. Ask for examples. Did deviates get rejected? What problems might the norms solve?

Think of some cases where conformity is desirable, and where it is undesirable.

Obedience and Persuasion

KEY AIMS: By the end of Part 3 you will have:
➢ learnt about classic experiments in which people obeyed orders to carry out antisocial acts;
➢ gained an understanding of why people obey orders from those in authority;
➢ learnt about research into the process of persuasion, and the effect of the design of the message, the source of the message, and the characteristics of the recipient, on persuasion;
➢ studied the social skills of assertiveness.

Obedience

This section is about ways in which one person can influence another, to change their behaviour, beliefs or attitudes. We start with obedience. This is where one person is in a position of some authority, and makes another do something which they may or may not want to do. This research was inspired by the behaviour of police and military in Nazi Germany who obeyed orders to carry out extremely antisocial acts.

Milgram's experiments

These are some of the most striking experiments in social psychology, and they produced some very interesting results. They can't be done again, because **ethics committees** no longer allow this sort of thing.

Milgram (1974) advertised for participants in a New Haven local paper, offering four dollars for people to take part in an experiment on human learning at Yale University in the USA. When they arrived, participants met what seemed to be another participant, a middle-aged man, who was actually an accomplice of the experimenter. They drew lots, and it was fixed so that the real participant drew the role of 'teacher', while the other, the 'learner' was to learn a series of word pairs, such as 'blue–sky'.

The 'learner' was then strapped into a chair and had electrodes attached to his arm (*see Figure* 3.1).

The teacher was shown how to use an electric shock machine, which was labelled from 15 to 450 volts as 'slight shock' to 'danger: severe shock' and finally 'XXX' and given a sample 45- volt shock. He was told that every time the learner made a mistake he should give him an electric shock, starting at 15 volts and increasing by 15 volts each time up to 450 volts. The learner was usually in the next room but could be clearly heard.

The learner made a series of pre-arranged mistakes, and was given some small shocks. The increasingly-agitated responses of the accomplice were carefully scripted, though of course he didn't actually receive any shocks at all. These responses were: at 120 volts, 'Ugh! Hey this really hurts'; at 150 volts, 'Ugh! Experimenter! That's all. Get me out of here. I told you I had heart trouble... Let me out'; at 270 volts he gave an agonized scream; at 310 volts, 'I told you

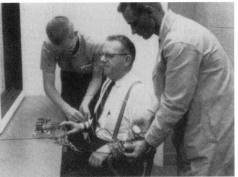

Figure 3.1: The photo on the left shows Stanley Milgram with the apparatus he used in in his famous experiments on obedience. The photo on the right shows the experimenter (right front) and a subject (rear) attaching electrodes to the learner's (accomplice's) wrists.

I refuse to answer. I am no longer part of the experiment'. When he refused to answer this was treated as a further error. The 'teacher' usually became very distressed, and became reluctant to give more shocks or appealed for guidance. The experimenter then used four degrees of orders from 'Please continue' to 'You have no choice, you must go on'.

The amazing result of this experiment was that 28 out of 40 males (65 per cent) went all the way to 450 volts, with an average maximum of 368 volts, and the female participants did the same (see *Figure* 3.2).

Milgram carried out several experimental variations to see if they would affect the degree of obedience of participants. These were:

1. *Physical closeness*. When the learner was in the same room, 40 per cent of participants went to 450 volts; when the teacher had to place the learner's hand on the shock plate it fell to 30 per cent, compared with 65 per cent when the victim was in the next room.

2. *Presence of authority*. Obedience fell to 21 per cent if the experimenter's commands came over the telephone, and there was a low level of obedience if the experimenter left the room and his role was taken over by a clerical assistant. If this person tried to take over giving the shocks, participants protested, some unplugged the machine, and one even threw him across the room. No one did this to the real experimenter.

3. *Status of the institution*. The obedience level was less if the experiment was moved from Yale University to an office down town called 'Research Associates of Bridgeport'.

4. *Peer group support*. When there was a second confederate who refused to go beyond 210 volts, only 10 per cent of the participants went to 450 volts. But if a second confederate went all the way, so did 92 per cent of the participants, compared with 65 per cent in the original experiment.

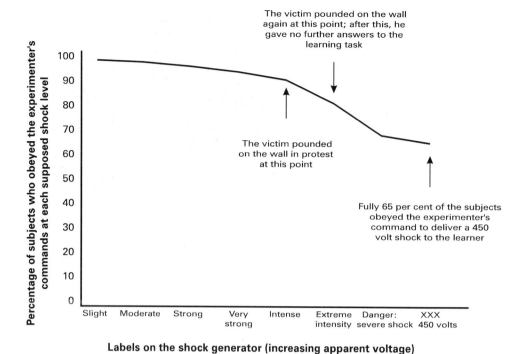

The victim pounded on the wall again at this point; after this, he gave no further answers to the learning task

The victim pounded on the wall in protest at this point

Fully 65 per cent of the subjects obeyed the experimenter's command to deliver a 450 volt shock to the learner

Labels on the shock generator (increasing apparent voltage)

Figure 3.2: As shown here, a surprisingly large proportion of the participants in Milgram's research obeyed the experimenter's orders to deliver electric shocks to increasing strength to an innocent victim. Fully 65 per cent demonstrated total obedience to these commands. (Source: based on data from Milgram, 1974.)

SAQ
10

Describe three conditions when people are most likely to be obedient.

What is the explanation for these extraordinary findings? The participants knew they were doing something wrong, and were obviously in states of considerable distress, so why did they carry on? Was it because they were mentally disturbed or criminal? There is no evidence for this, and in fact individual differences in personality had little effect on obedience, because the situational pressures were so strong. The following are some factors to consider.

1. Milgram's explanation is that we have all been rewarded as children for obedience and punished for disobedience, so being given an order by someone in authority switches on what he called the **agentic** mode of unthinking obedience. In the main, we have had further experience that most authorities are trustworthy.

2. There is a second factor which was built into the experiment. This was that the participants were gradually committed to their course of action and were on a slippery slope; by the time they got to 300 volts they had already given 20 shocks and it would be difficult and embarrassing to confront the experimenter and get out of the experiment.

3. The behaviour of the experimenter was probably important too. He behaved in an impersonal, objective way, and acted 'as if he is simply presenting the

social–moral world as he sees it' (Sabini, 1995). This is partly a matter of non-verbal communication – he is in charge and he doesn't seem to be at all worried, so things must be OK.

4. In military situations, such as Nazi Germany mentioned earlier, there is another reason for obedience – you are likely to be punished, perhaps executed, if you disobey. The interest of Milgram's experiment is that there is so much obedience *without* such danger of punishment.

SAQ 11

Give three possible reasons why so many of Milgram's participants behaved so badly.

It seems that all of us, or most of us, are capable of doing awful things if ordered to do so. So when are we able to resist such orders?

• When we have peer group support – this reduced obedience to 10 per cent in Milgram's experiment. Observing disobedient models is also effective.

• When we are reminded of our responsibility for any harm done, as later versions of this study have found.

• Having knowledge of experiments like these has been found to reduce obedience (Baron and Byrne, 1997).

Obedience in the outside world

Such incidents can happen in the real world too. Twenty-three nurses were ordered via a telephone call from someone who claimed to be a doctor, to administer an overdose of a drug. Twenty-two were about to do so until intercepted (Hofling *et al.*, 1966). Patients usually obey doctors to some extent, but on average they only take half the prescribed pills, and often ignore advice about smoking, drinking and so on. Members of religious cults often obey the orders of their leader, no matter how serious the consequence may be. In the most disastrous of these cases, 911 followers of the Reverend Jim Jones, all members of the People's Temple in Guyana, drank a lethal strawberry and cyanide mixture and died.

However, there is protest and disobedience as well as obedience, from the Newbury by-pass, hunt saboteurs and Greenham Common in the UK, to the demolition of the Berlin Wall and the collapse of communism in Eastern Europe.

Are there national differences in obedience? The Milgram experiment has been repeated in a number of countries with differing results. Some of the differences found may be due to the way the experiment was conducted; for example, what kind of people were used as subjects might make a difference. For what they are worth, the highest levels of obedience found have been in Holland (92 per cent), Spain (over 90 per cent), Italy and Germany (85 per cent), and Austria (80 per cent). America was 65 per cent. The lowest obedience scores were in Britain (50 per cent) and Australia (28 per cent). However, these were small groups of participants, often students, and in no way representative samples of the populations of these countries (Smith and Bond, 1993).

This experiment has not, as far as we know, been replicated in China. In the traditional Chinese family, a very high degree of obedience is demanded by parents, and generally accepted by children. This is described by Jung Chang in her famous book *Wild Swans*, and is still common in parts of Asia.

Zimbardo's prison study

This study was about the behaviour of those who demand obedience from others, such as prison guards/officers. It demonstrates another example of antisocial behaviour on the part of ordinary people as a result of social influences. Zimbardo built a mock prison in the basement of Stanford University Psychology Department, and 24 male students from all over North America signed up to participate in a study of prison life for $15 per day for two weeks. Half were chosen at random to be the 'prisoners' and were collected in real police cars, frisked, stripped, deloused and put in the prison. The other half were the prison guards, and issued with uniforms, truncheons, and black reflecting glasses.

The guards understood that they were entitled to use minimal force to restrain unruly prisoners; presumably they knew that it is not right to treat people in a degrading and humiliating way. However, what happened was horrific: the guards treated the prisoners very badly, and imposed many senseless rules and tasks. The prisoners rebelled and were put down brutally, punished by being made to do push-ups, sleep deprivation, tasks like cleaning the lavatories with their bare hands, making them use buckets in their rooms for lavatories, creating degradation and squalor.

The prisoners became so distressed that the experiment had to be terminated after six days instead of two weeks. Some of the prisoners had uncontrollable fits of crying and screaming. There were actually three styles of guard behaviour: some were kind and helpful, some were average – not helpful but not brutal either, and the third group started most of the brutality (Haney, Banks and Zimbardo, 1983).

What could explain this behaviour by the guards? None of them had criminal records, and they had been screened for any possible psychological disorders. The following may help to explain it.

- It was partly because they were simply playing the roles they had been assigned, and behaving as they thought prison guards normally did. They were conforming to the norms of prison guard behaviour as they saw them.

- When confronted by disobedient prisoners, they assumed that some degree of force or coercion was needed to control them; some used too much. This was another slippery slope of deteriorating behaviour, as in the Milgram experiment.

- In this and other studies it has been found that once victims have been degraded it is easy to see them as sub-human, so that their rights can be ignored.

SAQ
12

Why did many of Zimbardo's prison guards behave so badly?

There are some problems with Zimbardo's study. It is not clear what the hypothesis was, or whether it was confirmed. The behaviour of the guards was partly due to the ambiguous nature of their situation, and only some of them behaved badly – though the others apparently did nothing to restrain them.

(?) *Do laboratory experiments on obedience miss some of the features of real-life obedience, for example in military or cult settings?*

Persuasion

Let us look at the various ways in which one person, not necessarily in a position of authority, can persuade another to do something, or change their attitudes or beliefs. This may be done face-to-face, in a public meeting, through TV, or in some kind of brain-washing situation. We now know a lot about the conditions under which there is most influence, and these will be revealed later, but we will look first at the basic processes involved.

Processes of attitude change

Research interest has focused on the **cognitive processes** involved in attitude change. For example, Greenwald (1968) proposed that an individual's attitude will change if a communication produces a lot of favourable thoughts. A possible test of this theory is to ask recipients to list their thoughts after receiving a persuasive experimental message; it is found that when these thoughts are favourable there is more attitude change, but only when they have attended to the message carefully. Distraction prevents people from doing this and is found to reduce the effects of a communication, but only for strong arguments; the effect of weak arguments is enhanced by distraction. Petty *et al.* (1976) carried out an experiment in which the persuasive message was accompanied by distracting flashing lights. When there was a higher rate of flashing the effect of weak arguments was increased (see *Figure* 3.3).

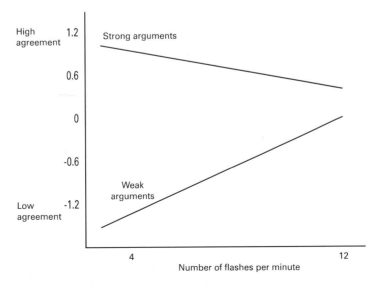

Figure 3.3: Mean attitude scores in relation to argument quality and level of distraction (Petty *et al.*, 1976).

This confirms the truth behind the old joke about the notes for a lecture saying 'Go quickly here – argument weak'.

A later development of this line of thinking is that there are two routes to persuasion. With good arguments and no flashing lights, people are able to study the message and be persuaded by it – the **central route**. But with weak arguments and distraction, they may be influenced more by the status or attractiveness of the sender, the glossiness of the documents, and other 'peripheral' features of the situation, not by the actual message. When the listener is personally involved in the issue, they take the central route, and are affected more by good arguments. Elaboration of the message takes place only when the central route is activated (Petty and Cacioppo, 1986).

The **peripheral/central route** distinction has been found to be very important. For example, when attitudes have been changed via the central route this lasts longer and is more resistant to later persuasion (Petty *et al.*, 1994).

Motivational processes may also be behind attitude change. Fear arousal was the main basis of evangelism in the eighteenth and nineteenth centuries – arouse fear of going to hell in your listeners and then tell them how to avoid this fate. This principle has been studied to see whether it helps in campaigns to stop people smoking, dental awareness weeks, or campaigns to increase safety on the roads. After many such experiments it is now clear that arousing fear does enhance attitude change, but only if:

- the danger is serious;
- the bad outcome is probable;
- the behaviour recommended will work; and
- the recipients are able to do what is asked (Maddux and Rogers, 1983).

It has sometimes been found that if the message is too frightening people will just not attend to it.

Advertisers make a lot of use of motivational arousal. They may suggest that their product will improve your health, social status, or sex life. This may involve some fear arousal, in connection with your health for example. They may offer a new self-image, as when the users of some kind of petrol are said to be 'get-away people' for example, or the users of the product are portrayed as glamorous, or upper class. The message has more effect if it is repeated up to three or four times, after which people get bored.

Religious cults and brain-washing, which have some similarities, use further processes of persuasion, and can have powerful effects on attitudes, though these effects often prove to be temporary. These effects include the production of a very high level of emotional arousal. Chinese thought reform, once practised on prisoners of war in Korea and on dissident intellectuals, used a 'struggle session' in which a candidate for conversion would be shouted at and shaken for many hours until he or she collapsed. Intense group pressure is part of the process, often including physical pressures. New members of cults are vulnerable to this kind of influence if they are in a state of social isolation and alienation; intense 'love' by the sect members has a powerful effect.

SAQ
13

Why should a verbal message, for example in an advertisement, influence someone's behaviour?

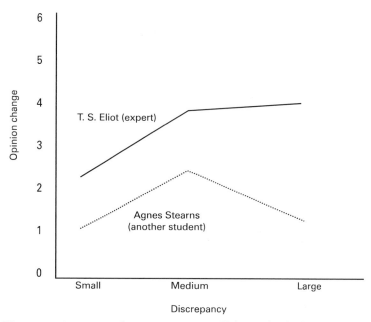

Figure 3.4: Discrepancy interacts with communicator credibility. Only a highly credible communicator maintains effectiveness when arguing an extreme position (from Aronson *et al.*, 1963, and redrawn by Myers, 1993).

Persuasive messages

The 'message', or communication, is at the centre of persuasion. We have seen that 'strong' arguments work better; that is, where there is a good argument or evidence, and this relates the desired behaviour, attitude or belief to other values or goals, or to clear needs. For example, 'Do this and it will preserve the environment; be good for the whales; help you get a job', are all strong arguments. The discrepancy between the position advocated and the initial position of the recipient should not be too large nor too small, though a large discrepancy may work with a highly credible communicator (Aronson *et al.*, 1963; see *Figure* 3.4).

Advertisers, for example on TV, use some different methods. The 'argument' may be mainly non-verbal, creating a visual link between, for example, being a very romantic kind of person and drinking a particular brand of coffee. There are no pictures of romantic people drinking other kinds of coffee or of non-romantic people drinking the advertised brand. The message is intended to modify the 'brand image'.

SAQ
14

Which kinds of messages are most persuasive?

SOMETHING TO TRY

Design an advert to persuade students to come to your school or college.

Persuasive people

Skills are needed to be persuasive. There are many experiments in which the persuasive effects of different kinds of communicator have been compared. It is found that communicators have more influence if:

- they have a forceful speech style, which is fast, expressive and fluent;
- they use dramatic examples, and sense of humour;
- they have powerful gestures and an assertive posture (Argyle, (1988).

These factors may explain the 'charisma' of some religious leaders. These skills are very important for those who do their persuading in public meetings, as they must be able to arouse the interest and excitement of the audience, and generate the right emotions for their cause.

Persuaders have more success when they are experts or are seen as experts. They do better if they are trusted, are seen as esteemed members of the group, and do not seem to be biased or pursuing their own ends, as advertisers are, for example. They do better if they are liked, and if they are seen to be a member of the group being addressed. Attractive persuaders do well, for example if they are physically attractive, or are well-known entertainers or athletes. Of course the communicator will do well if he or she has power over the recipient, but this takes us back to obedience.

The recipients

Some individuals are easier to persuade than others. Here are the main variables:

- *Age*. Those between 18–25 are more persuadable, as they have not made up their minds yet and do not have fixed ideas. However, there are no further changes with age; that is, the old do not become any more rigid.

- *Intelligence*. If the message is complex and well-argued, the more intelligent will be influenced more; if the argument is weak, the opposite occurs.

- *Expertise*. Those who are expert or well-informed about the topic of the message are influenced less.

- *Self-esteem*. People with low self-esteem are influenced more; those who have sudden religious conversions have often been in a state of distress or uncertainty.

- *Mood*. Those in a good mood are easier to influence, as they don't examine the arguments so carefully.

SAQ
15

Which kinds of people are most persuadable?

The channel

Passive reception of messages, as in advertisements and junk mail, has the weakest effect. Personal contact does better, as was found in a big study to reduce heart disease in three Californian towns. In two of them there was a two-year media campaign to change health behaviour like smoking, diet and exercise, and in the third, 'Watsonville', there were also personal visits by health professionals (see *Figure* 3.5).

Public meetings do better than the media, except that only the converted attend usually. However, they are motivated to influence other people, armed

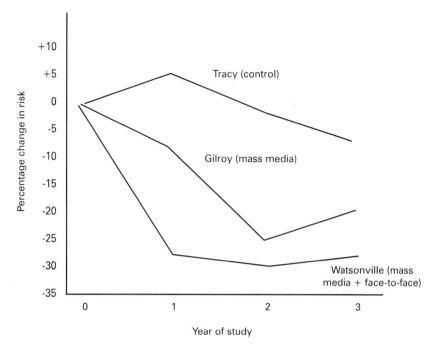

Figure 3.5: Percentage change from baseline (0) in coronary risk after one, two, or three years of health education (from Maccoby, 1980).

with new arguments and enthusiasm, which is known as the 'two-step model'; they act as opinion leaders (Katz, 1957).

Written messages can do well however, especially if the arguments are difficult and need to be studied.

Building in some rewards for the recipient is good, even if it is just giving them peanuts and a soft drink while reading the message. It is better if the behaviour required will actually be rewarding – for example, saving money.

There are other ways of changing attitudes apart from verbal persuasion. For example, negative attitudes to other groups, such as towards other races or colleges, can be modified by personal contact with members of that group, especially if the meeting is co-operative and on equal status terms. Wilder (1986) reports a successful attempt to change attitudes to members of a rival college by arranging meetings with members of it; when these students were said to be typical and were found to be pleasant, attitudes to that college changed (see *Figure* 3.6).

There are some special techniques which have been used in face-to-face situations. In one of these, the 'foot in the door' method, the influencer starts by making a very small request, such as asking a householder a few simple questions about the soap used in their home. When this was done, 53 per cent then agreed to a much bigger request to allow a large crew to search the house to do a product inventory. Only 22 per cent of those who had not received the large request first agreed (Freedman and Fraser, 1966). Another persuasive technique is the 'door in the face' approach. Here the persuader starts by making a ridiculously large request, for example, to do two hours a week

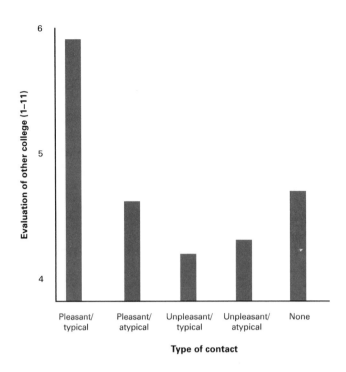

Figure 3.6: Evaluation of an outgroup after contact with a typical or atypical outgroup member (from Wilder, 1984).

looking after juvenile delinquents unpaid for two years. When the request was made (and of course refused), 50 per cent of respondents agreed to spend two hours taking the delinquents to the zoo, compared with 17 per cent of those who were approached cold (Cialdini *et al.*, 1975).

Describe a situation in which it might be easy to influence someone, and how you would go about it.

A POSSIBLE PROJECT

Design a campaign to stop people smoking.

Assertiveness

This is a general style of face-to-face social behaviour, which includes the capacity to exert influence and to avoid being influenced by others. It also includes the ability to say 'No', to stand up for oneself, ask favours, initiate and end encounters. Assertiveness training was originally introduced by behaviour therapists in the belief that this kind of behaviour inhibited anxiety. It may do so, but as we shall see, it has some other advantages.

Assertiveness can best be regarded as an important component of social skills, but it is not the whole of social skills, since it is only about influencing people, not about making friends. It is done by using the kinds of verbal requests and arguments already described, and, in addition the non-verbal style of dominance combined with sufficient warmth to be rewarding. The importance of the warm-and-dominant style is explained in another Unit in this series, *Social Relationships* (Argyle, 1998).

Assertiveness is quite different from aggressiveness, indeed, it is sometimes taught to violent offenders to show them how to exert influence without violence. Skilled social performers, and women more frequently than men, are assertive in a style which takes account of the needs and concerns of others, rather than just controlling their behaviour.

The main advantage of assertiveness is that it makes it possible to exert more influence in social situations. This can be very useful at work for teachers, managers, doctors and others. It can be useful for leisure, for running clubs for example. And it is useful with friends as they can be influenced without being upset. We have found that assertiveness is a cause of happiness, probably since it gives people more control over their lives. People can be trained in such skills by methods which are described later.

SAQ 17

Why can assertiveness be a useful social skill?

SOMETHING TO TRY

1. *Videotape a TV commercial. List some of the persuasive techniques used. What else could they have done?*
2. *Videotape a political speech. What social skills are being used? How might this person's skills be improved?*

Is it always desirable to be assertive?

Leadership

> KEY AIMS: By the end of Part 4 you will:
> ➤ *be aware of the difference between emergent and appointed leaders;*
> ➤ *have found out about the skills of effective leaders;*
> ➤ *have found out about second line leaders and above;*
> ➤ *see how leaders can be trained.*

The emergence of leaders

Let us look at the question of what type of person emerges as the leader of an otherwise leaderless group. Many studies have been done to find this out. The most important factor turns out to be having the skills, expertise or knowledge which will help the whole group to succeed in whatever it is trying to do. So, if the group is playing football, being good at football is important; if it is involved in crime, there are other skills which are more relevant. If the group sometimes plays football and sometimes engages in crime, the leadership will change, depending on what they are doing. The groups studied were all informal groups, where the leader had no official position and had little power to reward or punish.

In research on juries it has been found, in the past at least, that the foreman more or less elects him or herself – it is often a middle class, middle-aged male,

Figure 4.1: A political meeting. Is there a particular kind of personality which makes people leaders?

32

who has some assertive skills (Strodtbeck *et al.*, 1958). He or she often starts by sitting in a central position, saying, 'Who's going to be the foreman?'. Is there a particular kind of personality which makes people leaders? Certain features have often been found to be correlated with becoming a leader, but the statistical strength of these relationships is very weak. These features are:

* intelligence
* height
* need to dominate or have power
* the capacity to adjust to different situations – self-monitoring (described earlier)

However, it should be emphasized that these are weak predictors, and that having the most useful skills or knowledge is more important.

Sometimes a leader needs to emerge quickly, as with juries and some committees. What happens then is that in the initial talk some members get down to business straight away and talk about the task – they are, in a sense, the candidates for leadership. The others then approve or disapprove of what these candidates say, both verbally, by agreeing or disagreeing, and non-verbally, by smiling and nodding or groaning and shaking their heads. This reinforcement causes some of the candidates to talk more, others less, and the rewarded ones become the leaders of the group (Hollander, 1985).

SAQ
\18/

What kind of person is likely to emerge as the leader of a group?

There is often a second leader of a different kind, sometimes referred to as the **socio-emotional leader**. This person is more concerned with the welfare of the group than with its task; he, or more often she, is good at bringing in those who are left out, smoothing out disputes, and generally maintaining the cohesion of the group (Wilke and Van Knippenberg, 1996).

SAQ
\19/

What are the differences between emergent and appointed leaders?

The skills of appointed leaders

Most leaders are appointed in some way, and not by the group itself; for example, with teachers, team captains, industrial supervisors and managers, army officers and NCOs (non-commissioned officers). All of these occupy a position in an organizational hierarchy, and have some power to reward and punish, which informal leaders do not have. These leaders have a big effect on the success of their group, such as whether or not the team wins, or how much work a group produces. The question now is which kinds of leaders are most successful? It depends most on their style of leadership and the kind of leadership skills they use.

Three aspects of leadership style have been found to be important.

1. Instructing and organizing
This is the central job of the leader. A scale for measuring the extent to which they do it, using ratings by 'subordinates', includes items like:

- decides what shall be done and how it shall be done
- schedules the work to be done
- lets group members know what is expected of them (Fleishman, 1953).

However, these essential tasks must be done very carefully, because people generally don't like being ordered about. It is sometimes better to use suggestions or questions, particularly if the subordinates are highly skilled; for example, if they are research workers.

2. Rewardingness

If the first dimension corresponds to the activities of an emergent leader, the 'task leader', this second one corresponds to the socio-emotional leader. This is about looking after and rewarding the group members. A scale for measuring it includes items like:

- is friendly and approachable
- looks out for the personal welfare of group members

These scales have been widely used in research on leadership.

The two dimensions just described are very important in producing effective groups, and they are needed in combination – the subordinates should be told what to do and then rewarded if they do it.

These styles of leadership also have a big impact on the members' 'job satisfaction'. In industrial settings, when satisfaction is low, the members are likely to be absent more, or simply leave. This is called 'labour turnover' in industry. *Figure* 4.2 shows the effect of these two dimensions on labour turnover. It can be seen that it can be four times as high if 'consideration' (our rewardingness) is too low, or if 'initiating structure' (instructing and organizing) is too high.

There is another, third, dimension of leadership skills.

3. Participatory leadership

This is the extent to which a leader consults members of the group, or the group as a whole. Real social skills are needed to be able to consult a group, arrive at a useful decision, and get the group committed to carrying it out. This kind of leader doesn't just tell people what to do, he or she involves them in the decision and thus persuades them that they want to do it.

This style goes well with generally democratic and consultative social organizations, where people are elected to offices or committees, as happens in many leisure organizations, universities and industries which have brought in some 'industrial democracy'. On the other hand, I have recently found that in some sports groups, choirs, and voluntary work bodies there is no democracy at all, in that there is no elected committee, and no regular way of changing the leadership. However, I also discovered that often the other members don't care – they don't want to spend time running the club, they just want to play tennis (Argyle, 1996)!

These three aspects of leadership skills are applicable to a wide variety of settings, though what is actually done by an army sergeant, a team captain and a teacher is rather different. In addition, the optimal style varies somewhat with the situation. For example, if the group members are having a bad time in some

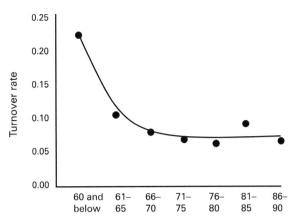

Figure 4.2(a): Consideration.

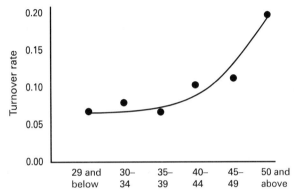

Figure 4.2(b): Initiating structure (from Fleishman and Harris, 1962). Note: the horizontal scale gives scores on the dimensions 'Consideration' and 'Initiating structure'.

way, they will need more of the rewardingness dimension to keep them going. If the task is difficult or unclear they need more of the instructions dimension. If leaders are not sure what decision to take, or suspect that the group may not accept their decision, then is the time to increase participation. But sometimes there is no time for discussion or persuasion, as in some military situations or in the middle of a sports event.

Under which conditions are each of the three aspects of leadership skills – instruction, reward and participation - most important?

A further element of leadership skills has recently been discovered – **charismatic leadership**. There are some individuals who can communicate a new vision or mission, and can inspire a group to pursue new goals. Such leaders have been found to be effective in times of crisis, when a new or challenging task needs to be done, as, for example, in the case of the new leader of a political party (Howell and Frost, 1989).

What verbal and non-verbal skills might be used by a charismatic leader?

Second-line leaders

First-line leaders, such as teachers and industrial supervisors, come under the direction of **second-line leaders**, for example, heads of departments and head teachers. These need similar skills to those of first-line leaders, and some extra ones. They need the skills of managing an organization, with its administrative structures and committees, skills of public relations and dealing with the public, of addressing large meetings, interviewing job applicants, chairing committees, and perhaps negotiating with trade unions (Argyle, 1989).

Hierarchies with second-line leaders and above have some problems. These leaders need to know what is happening at the 'coal-face', but to find out how an individual at the lowest level is feeling, or thinking, or getting on, normally means going through the first line leader, so that four communications are needed to get the answer. It is worse than this since upward communications may be delayed until each senior person is thought to be in a receptive mood. The information may also be improved in order to maintain the reputation of the senders.

Training for leadership

We have seen that some leaders are much more effective than others. Industrial supervision was the first social skill to be analysed to show the measurable consequences of using different styles of behaviour. If it is known which skills are most successful, these can be taught. Such training is now given to those who are doing a wide variety of jobs, including supervisors and managers, doctors and nurses, teachers and clergy, and many others.

The extent of the need for such training is shown by the differences between good and bad performers. *Figure* 4.1 showed that some industrial supervisors can produce four times as much labour turnover as others. Some can produce eight times as much absenteeism. We found that some sales people regularly sell four times as much as others. Some teachers are unable to keep order, some survey interviewers get a lot of refusals. It has been found in firms who send their staff abroad, that sometimes as many as 60 per cent of staff cannot cope with the new culture, and have to come home; this is common for those posted to the Far or Middle East, unless they have been trained.

In a companion Unit in this series, *Social Relationships* (Argyle, 1998), we describe the problems of those who have no friends, or who can't cope with the opposite sex, or who can't stay married. These are all disasters for those concerned, but these individuals too can be trained.

Follow-up studies of training schemes for teachers, managers, interviewers, doctors and others have shown very positive effects of Social Skills Training (SST), and it is now widely used for many kinds of people at work. Eighty per cent of teachers in Britain receive some microteaching, for example, – that is, trainee teachers teach a class of 5–6 pupils for 15 minutes, and are then given feedback on their performance, including playing back a video of the session. There have been some notable successes at a higher level too, for example, during a US presidential election when Jimmy Carter was trained to use a more assertive non-verbal style in his debates with Gerald Ford.

SAQ 21

What problems do second-line leaders have?

?

How far can a leader allow his or her followers to participate in decisions?

Crowds and Collective Behaviour

A **crowd** is defined as 'a large number of people gathered together, usually without orderly arrangement' (the *Concise Oxford Dictionary*). Familiar examples are football crowds, political marches and demonstrations, race riots, some religious meetings, some concerts and strikes. These all differ in a number of ways, and crowds are therefore difficult to classify. Roger Brown (1954) divided them into *mobs*, which are active, and *audiences*, which are passive. He divided mobs into:

- *aggressive mobs*, such as those involved in lynchings and other riots
- *escape mobs*, as in crowds of people rushing away from something in panic
- *acquisitive mobs*, as in those involved in looting
- *expressive mobs*, including religious, political and football crowds

Some crowds are noisy and uncontrolled, but others are quite peaceful, as with most cricket matches, many concerts and church services.

Crowds can also be classified according to how large they are, whether there is a leader or concealed leader, and whether there are official controls to keep them in order.

Size is probably an important variable. The larger the crowd, the more anonymous, and perhaps the more powerful, individual members will feel.

Crowds also vary in **density**, that is, the number of people per square yard. Crowds have certain **shapes**. A common one is the ring, with the leader or other centre of interest in the middle. Those who are more actively engaged, and those who get there early, will be nearer the middle. Another kind of crowd has the main performers at the front, and the rest forming an audience. Some crowds are on the move, as in marches.

In both these kinds of crowds there is some degree of **polarization**, that is, focusing of attention, on certain individuals or events. The degree of polarization can be calculated from the proportion of individuals who are looking at the central actors. In some crowds, such as race riots and football crowds, the focus of attention is on the enemy, who may be the police or opposing fans.

However, within a crowd there may be **subgroups**, and some may not be very interested in the main activity. The composition of a crowd is important. There may be leaders, visible or concealed, keen supporters of whatever the crowd has gathered about, half-hearted supporters, those who are actually against it, and aggressive and disturbed individuals who are there 'for the aggro' (Milgram and Toch, 1969).

Some rioting crowds are precipitated by a single event, for example a race riot after a rape or murder, or allegations of police brutality. In addition, there may be long-term causes, such as feelings of economic injustice or other long-held resentments. Some crowds, such as football crowds, begin as organized and peaceful affairs, and then something happens to disturb it and violence breaks out.

Methods for studying crowds

At first sight it seems very difficult to do research on crowds, but several methods have been used with some success.

1. *Observation*. This has been the traditional method, as used by Le Bon (1895), for example. It has also been used by later investigators, for example Marsh *et al.* (1978) in their study of football crowds.

2. *Interviews*. Several investigators have used interviews. For example, Reicher (1984) interviewed some of those involved in a race riot in Bristol which had been triggered by the police searching some black youths for drugs (see also p. 42). However, no one has so far been able to carry out a proper sample survey of a crowd. Marsh also interviewed some of his football fans, and gave them some cognitive tests to find how they saw the sub-groups of fans, and to identify which uniforms they wore.

3. *Experiments*. We have seen that this is the preferred method in social psychology, but that the main drawback to this is the danger of being unrealistic. French (1944) tried to produce a panic by locking his participants in a room and releasing smoke into it. However, it did not result in the desired panic, perhaps because the participants were accustomed to deceptions being used in social psychology experiments at that time. More successful have been a series of experiments on **de-individuation**; that is, concealing identity by dressing participants in overalls and hoods to see if it makes them more aggressive. The results of these experiments will be discussed shortly. You might also consider how far laboratory experiments can reproduce crowd phenomena.

4. *Field experiments*. These would provide more realistic evidence if they could be done, and if ethics committees would allow it. One which was allowed was by Sherif *et al.* (1961), the famous 'Robber's cave' study. A group of 11–12-year-old boys at a summer camp was divided into separate huts, and competed in games, leading to strong in-group feelings and a dangerous level of hostility between the groups. This was resolved by getting the groups to work together for shared goals, such as restoring the deliberately disrupted water supply.

Le Bon's account of crowds

The study of crowds began with the observations by Le Bon (1895), based on the behaviour of crowds in the French Revolution and in later violent street mobs in Paris. His observations were anecdotal and unscientific, and were motivated by the desire to keep the working class masses down, but they have been the basis for much later research.

Le Bon thought that crowds exerted a powerful effect on their members, making them become homogeneous, and forming a 'collective mind', which made them irrational and primitive in their thinking, lose self-control, and left them open to becoming intensely emotional and aggressive under the influence of fanatical leaders.

He thought that three processes were responsible for this behaviour:

1   *anonymity*, leading to loss of responsibility and feeling of power;
2   *contagion*, almost like an infectious disease being caught;
3   *suggestibility*, that is, uncritical acceptance of what one is told to do, like hypnotism.

Le Bon's observations have been very influential but they have also been criticized. An alternative to the idea that crowds transform people is the idea of **convergence**, that violent norms are produced by the kind of people who turn up as part of the crowd. We have already seen that not all crowds are violent or uncontrolled. Individuals can be emotional and aggressive all by themselves. And it remains to be seen whether the mechanisms he postulated actually work in crowds.

SAQ
22

What did Le Bon think were the three main features of crowds?

Freud's explanation of crowd behaviour

Freud (1922) was greatly influenced by Le Bon, and accepted his account of crowd behaviour. He wanted to explain the irrational nature of crowd behaviour in terms of unconscious processes, and argued that crowd members form strong ties with each other, based on their shared identification with the leader, where they replace their own **superegos** with the leader. They regress to child-like dependency on him or her, and have no internal restraints; any restraints will come from the leader. The result is homogeneity between members, based on shared ideals, and strong ties between them.

This account explains the remarkable power of the leaders of some religious cults, as we have seen, and of some political leaders. It is similar to Milgram's idea of the agentic mode where there is uncritical acceptance of a leader's orders, and it has been rediscovered by the anthropologist Victor Turner (1967), who described the behaviour of groups of young men in African primitive society undergoing initiation rites into manhood. They too are dependent on the leader, in this case the priest, and they form very strong bonds with each other, and experience a state of love and equality, which he called **communitas**. On the other hand, there are crowds, which are equally irrational and violent, which have no leader, or at any rate no visible leader. And it must be admitted that there is no hard empirical evidence in support of these ideas. We shall see later that larger crowds tend to be more aggressive, but other theories can explain this too.

SAQ
23

How did Freud explain the special features of crowds?

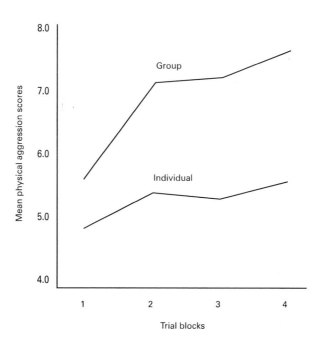

Figure 5.1: Escalation of physical aggression for individuals and groups (from Jaffe and Yinon, 1983).

De-individuation

One of the most active areas of crowd research also follows from Le Bon – the idea that members of crowds experience a loss of self-awareness and individual identity and thus feel less responsible for what they do. De-individuation was first assessed by self-report and was found to correlate with willingness to criticize participants' parents. Several conditions have been found to increase de-individuation:

Size. There can be more anti-social behaviour in a larger group. Mann (1981) analysed 21 cases where a crowd encouraged a potential suicide to jump; crowds were more likely to do this when the crowd was large, and if it was under cover of darkness – again, a source of anonymity. Jaffe and Yinon (1983) did a laboratory experiment in which participants were angered by a confederate. Groups of participants gave the confederate larger shocks later than did individual participants, so there is some support for the view that groups are aggressive, given the same provocation (see *Figure*. 5.1).

Gergen *et al*. (1973) put 14 students, seven of each sex, initially strangers, in a totally dark room for an hour. Their behaviour was totally different from that when the lights were on – there was a great deal of bodily contact and intimate behaviour in the dark.

Group unity. Diener (1979) generated de-individuation by organizing groups of eight, of whom six were confederates, who sang and swayed together in unison, with the result that the real subjects reported feeling less self-conscious, acting more spontaneously and engaging in more uninhibited behaviour.

Surveillance and accountability. Participants in experiments give larger electric shocks if they think they will not meet the victim later, and people are more likely to be anti-social if there is no surveillance of their behaviour.

41

List three factors that contribute to a state of 'de-individuation'.

Convergent and emergent norms in crowds

According to Le Bon and others, members of crowds influence each other by a kind of *contagion*, like people catching a disease from each other, and this is a circular process which intensifies the original ideas and feelings. There is plenty of research showing that people can influence each other's ideas and feelings in this way.

Another version of this is to emphasize the **convergence** that results, arguing that the crowd forms norms in the usual way, formed from the initial ideas and behaviour of its members. So any anti-social behaviour would be due to the anti-social composition of the crowd, and disorderly crowd behaviour blamed on the disorderly individuals in it.

Emergent norm theory is quite different and argues that crowds develop new norms. But it is also said that these norms are an illusion and that most of the members of what seems to be an aggressive crowd are in fact only interested bystanders. This illusion of the crowd norms is created by the visible behaviour of a few individuals, and by the circulation of rumours (Turner, 1974). There is some degree of social control in crowds, based on contacts between individuals who know each other, and the process of norm formation just described.

This theory can describe why there should be shifts of norms in crowds, but doesn't explain the direction in which they will shift (Hogg and Abrams, 1988).

Race riots and Social Identity Theory

This account starts from the observation that there are clearly norms in many crowds, such as those of football fans, which we shall describe later. But how is there such conformity if there is loss of self-awareness? And why is there such a degree of conformity despite the existence of very different sub-groups? Reicher (1984) proposed that what happens in a crowd is a shift in self-identity to a shared identity with other members of the crowd. They learn what the proper behaviour is which shows they are group members, such as wearing the right clothes. The norms are derived from the occasion for the crowd's existence, such as opposition to the police.

Social identity theory offers an explanation of 'inter-group behaviour'; that is, behaviour of members of one group towards members of another. It proposes that there is a drive to enhance self-esteem, that self-esteem depends partly on shared **social identity** based on memberships of groups and much inter-group conflict is due to attempts to enhance the position of such groups.

Reicher supported this theory by experiments in which it was found that when membership of a group was made salient, for example as 'social science students' members of laboratory groups expressed more anti-vivisection attitudes, which they thought were typical in this group. Reicher carried out a very interesting study of a race riot in Bristol in 1980. Police had searched black youths for drugs rather aggressively – the suppression of cannabis had been a long-standing source of annoyance. The result was a serious riot, in which police cars were overturned and set on fire, and policemen attacked, led by older black youths, but involving both black and white members of the community. Interviews with some of those involved showed that they were united in their opposition to the police as an oppressive and illegitimate authority, and that there was considerable cohesion in the community. This was not an uncontrolled riot at all, the main target being the police, not property, it was kept within the immediate area, and the crowd kept traffic flowing and prevented damage to domestic property. Like some other riots it was triggered by a small event, and suddenly exploded, probably because of the already existing feelings of frustration at not being able to control their own life style and of being dealt with by the police in a disrespectful manner. This was a highly polarized crowd, against the police.

This is an interesting theory, though there is not much hard evidence yet in support of it. It does not perhaps do justice to the irrationality and the aggressiveness of some crowds, as described by Le Bon, and the concern of some of the other theories.

SAQ 25

What does social identity theory say about crowd behaviour?

Football crowds

These are probably the largest, and sometimes most troublesome, crowds in Britain nowadays. On several occasions large numbers of fans have been killed, due to walls or stands collapsing, mainly as a result of crowds being out of control. These crowds consist of two polarized groups, with intense rivalry and hostility towards each other. The two groups of supporters gather separately before the match, threaten and insult each other during the match, sometimes charging and attacking each other in large groups, invading the pitch, fighting each other outside the ground afterwards, and causing miscellaneous damage. The two groups of fans are separated in different parts of the ground, and are restrained by large numbers of police.

Since the battles are between two groups of very similar individuals, who have not done anything to each other, what is the battle actually about? Social identity theory would say that they are fighting to increase their self-esteem, to enhance their identity by putting down members of the other group. Football fans are clearly identified with their teams, which seems to be very important for them, and they want to enhance their reputation to the detriment of the other side. Status is gained either by the team winning, or, failing this, by humiliating supporters of the other side. The insults used are mainly to the effect that the other side are weak, non-masculine, 'wankers', and so on.

Despite occasional disasters, most football crowds are not really very aggressive. Marsh *et al.* (1978) argued that they are engaging only in symbolic aggression, in the form of insults and the like, and that few actually get hurt. Marsh interviewed many fans and found that their aim was more to frighten the other side, or make them look ridiculous, rather than to injure them; indeed there were rules to this effect. Police statistics also show very few injuries at football matches. However, it is widely believed that football 'hooligans' are very dangerous, and they enjoy this reputation, mainly created by the press, of being dangerous and violent: 'We are the famous football hooligans'. However, it must by admitted that Marsh's work was mainly done at the Oxford United ground, and at more important matches, especially international ones, there is sometimes more serious trouble.

Marsh, and later Morris (1981), pursued the analogy between football fans and savage tribes. In both cases there are elaborate symbols of group membership; in this case, of scarves, badges, flags, and special ways of wearing clothes. There are elaborate rituals in the form of chants and processions. Anthropologists believe that rituals have the function of enhancing social cohesion, and this looks like a very good example of this process. Marsh also found that there is a hierarchy of sub-groups who occupy special positions in the stands, and that there is a 'career' as fans get older and accepted as genuine hooligans. There are other sub groups, including 'nutters', violent individuals who go for the fighting rather than the football, and who do not follow the rule of avoiding injuring people.

Much of Marsh and Morris' theory is consistent with social identity theory, but it adds more – the rules restraining aggression, the rituals and the sub-groups.

Elias and Dunning (1986), two sociologists, looked at a different aspect of football crowds – the social origins of the members. They found that nearly all football hooligans, such as the ones convicted of violence at matches, are unskilled or unemployed young men. They come from areas where parents do not restrain aggressive behaviour, the children often see fights between adults, and where 'macho' behaviour and 'hardness' are valued as the main source of reputation and status. Many of these young people have failed to achieve any success in either education or jobs, and turn to aggro as an alternative sphere of achievement and reputation.

Figure 5.2: Rival football fans (from Morris, 1981).

Some of the real hooligans enjoy fighting, as the following interview showed:

> I go to a match for one reason only: the aggro. It's an obsession, I can't give it up. I get so much pleasure when I'm having aggro that I nearly wet my pants … I go all over the country looking for it … every night during the week we go around the town looking for trouble. Before a match we go round looking respectable…then if we see someone who looks like the enemy we ask him the time; if he answers in a foreign accent, we do him over; and if he's got any money we roll him as well.
> (Elias and Dunning, 1986)

There are often feuds and vendettas between families and neighbourhoods, and it is suggested that this results in close bonding within these groups, and rejection of outsiders. This can explain why there is such aggressive rivalry between fans from different clubs – they come from different towns and support different teams. Elias and Dunning suggest that there has been a progressive civilizing of society since the Middle Ages, with improved manners and greater control of emotions in Britain. Sports have become less violent and better controlled. However, these civilising processes and better manners have not yet reached those involved in football hooliganism.

The Elias and Dunning account of football crowds is different from that of Marsh and Morris. It draws attention to the social origins and sub-culture from which violent fans are drawn and to historical processes. Marsh and Morris on the other hand point to the just-controlled violence, the rituals which bind these groups together, the costumes and chants which proclaim their identity. Both accounts agree that enhancing self-esteem and identity are important here, though they were developed independently of social identity theory.

Religious crowds

Some religious groups can be regarded as 'crowds', in that some of them are very large and uninhibited, and some display extraordinary behaviour. Others are more peaceful, though they may exhibit a lot of emotional arousal. Religion has always been a group affair, and in the most primitive kind of religion, shamanism, those present are worked up into states of hysterical arousal by means of very loud drumming, exhausting dancing, men in masks dressed as monsters or spirits, flames and darkness. In the time of John Wesley (the English preacher who founded Methodism, 1703–1791), people would get so carried away that they grovelled on the floor and barked like dogs. In the more recent 'Toronto Blessing', many become so aroused that they collapse on the floor. This form of service has the effect that many of the congregation become highly aroused, laugh uncontrollably, make animal-like noises, and collapse unconscious on the floor.

Religious groups are different from the crowds we have been discussing so far. They are certainly not aggressive. They appear to be uninhibited, in that they may behave in very unusual ways. However, these unusual ways are those prescribed by the leader or are norms of the group. Consider Pentecostalism, where 'speaking with tongues' is common. There is strong pressure to do this, and members may be given instruction in how to do it. Collapsing unconscious may appear to be spontaneous, but there is a remarkable similarity in how it is done in the Toronto Blessing.

A common factor in these groups is the generation of high levels of physiological arousal, or excitement. This is partly done by music, which may be very loud, and very emotional. There are often dramatic rituals, such as sacrifices in earlier religions, symbolic sacrifices to-day. In Tennessee and Carolina there are snake handling sects; passing rattlesnakes round produces a high level of terror. And the message from the preacher can be very arousing; for example, Billy Graham saying 'In 10 years' time a quarter of you will be dead'. John Wesley warned people of the proximity of Hell, which he told his hearers was 'about eighteen miles from here, straight down, in the bowels of the earth'. We discussed the phenomena of conformity and obedience in religious sects earlier.

The sheer number of people present adds to the power of religious meetings. Statistics from the Billy Graham organization show the percentages 'making decisions' at different meetings, going up to 5.3 per cent at the biggest meetings at Wembley (see *Table* 5.1).

Table 5.1 Percentages of audiences responding at Billy Graham's meetings (Beit-Hallahmi and Argyle, 1997)

	Average size of meeting	Number of meetings	Percentage making decisions
Graham Harringay meetings 1954 First four weeks	11,600	33	2.30
Relay services during 1954 campaign	930	430	0.44
Meetings addressed by members of Graham's team 1954	410	425	1.15
Graham's Glasgow meetings 1955	16,000	16	2.39
Graham's Wembley meetings 1955	56,000	8	5.30

These crowds are different from the others discussed so far in that they depend much more on the powers of individual leaders. Some religious leaders, like John Wesley and Billy Graham, had the skills which enabled them to captivate and arouse large audiences by the contents of their message, and by the non-verbal manner of its delivery.

Certain kinds of person may be more amenable to these kinds of influence. Studies of 'sudden' conversions have found that those converted in this way are usually young, and in a state of anxiety, guilt or uncertainty, and that the conversion puts them in a better frame of mind. Studies of those who joined sects which started in the 1960s, like the Moonies, find that those who joined were alienated, had left their families, and were often on drugs. They were offered intense 'love' and social support by these groups.

How do the theories of crowds discussed earlier fit religious groups? There is no aggression. There is loss of inhibition, but only in the ways prescribed by the group. There are certainly new norms, but these have emerged already and are imposed on new members. There is a change of identity on the part of those converted, but not only as members of a different group, more as better and less sinful persons. The special features of religious groups are the intense emotional arousal, the dependence on the leader, and the special methods of enhancing religious feelings, music and ritual.

What are the main differences between church and football crowds?

What features are shared by all kinds of crowds? Are there any theories which apply to all kinds of crowds?

REFERENCES

ALLEN, V.L. and LEVINE, J.M. (1971). Social support and conformity: the role of independent assessment of reality. *Journal of Experimental Social Psychology*, 7, 48–58.

ARGYLE, M. (1975; 1988). *Bodily Communication*. London: Methuen.

ARGYLE, M. (1987). Rules for relationships in four cultures. *Australian Journal of Psychology*, 38, 309–18.

ARGYLE, M. (1989). *The Social Psychology of Work*, 2nd edition. London: Penguin.

ARGYLE, M. (1994). *The Psychology of Interpersonal Behaviour*, 5th edition. London: Penguin.

ARGYLE, M. (1996). *The Social Psychology of Leisure*. London: Penguin.

ARGYLE, M. (1998). *Social Relationships*. Leicester: BPS Books (The British Psychological Society).

ARONSON, E., TURNER, J.A. and CARLSMITH, J.M. (1963). Communicator credibility and communicator discrepancy as determinants of opinion change. *Journal of Abnormal and Social Psychology*, 67, 31–36.

ASCH, S. E. (1956). Studies of independence and conformity: a minority of one against a unanimous majority. *Psychological Monographs*, 70, (Whole No.416).

AUSTIN, J. (1962). *How to do Things with Words*. Oxford: Oxford University Press.

BARON, R. A. and BYRNE, D. (1997). *Social Psychology: Understanding Human Interaction*, 8th edition. Boston: Allyn and Bacon.

BEIT-HALLAHMI, B. and ARGYLE, M. (1997). *The Psychology of Religious Behaviour, Belief and Experience*. London: Routledge.

BROWN, R.W. (1954). Mass phenomena. in G. Lindzey (Ed.) *Handbook of Social Psychology*, Vol.2. Cambridge, MA.: Addison-Wesley.

BUEHLER, R. and GRIFFIN, D. (1994). Change-of-meaning effects in conformity and dissent: observing construal processes over time. *Journal of Personality and Social Psychology*, 67, 984–96.

CHANG, J. (1993). *Wild Swans*. London: Flamingo.

CIALDINI, R.B. (1975). Reciprocal concessions procedure for inducing compliance: the door-in-the-face technique. *Journal of Personality and Social Psychology*, 31, 206–15.

CIALDINI, R.B., VINCENT, J.E., LEWIS, S.K., CATALAN, J., WHEELER, D. and DARBY, B.L. (1975). Reciprocal concessions procedure for inducing compliance: the foot-in-the-door technique. *Journal of Personality and Social Psychology*, 31, 206–15.

CRANDALL, C.S. (1988). Social contagion of binge eating. *Journal of Personality and Social Psychology*, 55, 882–94.

DIENER, E.. (1979). De-individuation, self-awareness and disinhibition. *Journal of Personality and Social Psychology*, 37, 1160-71.

EAGLY, A.H. and WOOD, W. (1982). Inferred sex differences in status as a determinant of gender stereotypes about social influence. *Journal of Personality and Social Psychology*, 43, 915–928.

EKMAN, P. and FRIESEN, W.V. (1969). Non-verbal leakage and clues to deception. *Psychiatry*, 32, 88–106.

EKMAN, P. and FRIESEN, W.V. (1975). *Unmasking the Face*. Englewood Cliffs, NJ: Prentice-Hall.

ELIAS, N. and DUNNING, E (1986). *The Quest for Excitement*. Oxford: Blackwell.

FESTINGER, L, RIECKEN, H.W. and SCHACHTER, S. (1956). *When Prophecy Fails*. Minneapolis: University of Minnesota Press.

FLANDERS, N.A. (1970). *Analyzing Teaching Behavior*. Reading, MA: Addison-Wesley.

FLEISHMAN, E.A. (1953). The description of supervisory behavior. *Journal of Applied Psychology*, 37, 1–6.

FLEISHMAN, E.A. and HARRIS, E.F. (1962). Patterns of leadership behavior related to employee grievances and turnover. *Personnel Psychology*, 15, 43–56.

FREEDMAN, J.L. and FRASER, S.C. (1966). Compliance without pressure: the foot-in-the-door technique. *Journal of Personality and Social Psychology*, 4, 195–202.

FRENCH, J.R.P. (1944). Organised and unorganised groups under fear and frustration. *University of Iowa Studies in Child Welfare*, 20, 229–308.

FREUD, S. (1922). *Group Psychology and the Analysis of the Ego*. London: Hogarth Press.

GERGEN, K.J., GERGEN, M. M. and BARTON, W.N. (1973). Deviance in the dark. *Psychology Today*, 129–130.

GILES, H. and COUPLAND, N. (1991). *Language, Contexts and Consequences*. Milton Keynes: Open University Press.

GREENWALD, A.G. (1968). Cognitive learning, cognitive response to persuasion, and attitude change. In A G. Greenwald, T.C., Brock, and T.M. Ostrom (Eds) *Psychological Foundations of Attitudes*. San Diego, CA.: Academic Press.

HANEY, C., BANKS, W. and ZIMBARDO, P. (1983). Interpersonal dynamics in a simulated prison. *International Journal of Criminology*, 1, 69-97.

HOFLING, C.K., BROTZMAN, E., DAIRYMPLE, S., GRAVES, N. and PIERCE, C.M. (1966). An experimental study in nurse–physician relationships. *Journal of Nervous and Mental Disease*, 143, 171–180.

HOGG, M.A. and ABRAMS, D. (1988). *Social Identifications*. London: Routledge.

HOLLANDER, E.P. (1985). Leadership and power. In G. Linzey and E. Aronson (Eds) *Handbook of Social Psychology, 3rd edition*. New York: Random House.

HOWELL, J.M. and FROST, P.J. (1989). A laboratory study of charismatic leadership. *Organizational Behavior and Human Decision Processes*, 43, 232–269.

JAFFE, Y. and YINON, Y. (1983). Collective aggression: the group–individual paradigm in the study of collective antisocial behavior. In H. H. Blumberg, A.P. Hare, V. Kent and M. H. Davies (Eds), *Small Groups and Social Interaction, Vol. 1*. Cambridge, MA.: Wiley.

KATZ, E. (1957). The two-step flow of communication: an up-to-date report on a hypothesis. *Public Opinion Quarterly*, 21, 61–78.

KENDON, A. (1967). Some functions of gaze direction in social interaction. *Acta Psychologica*, 28:1, 1–47.

LE BON, G. (1895). *The Crowd* (translated 1903). London: Unwin.

LINDE, C. (1988). The quantitative study of communicative success: politeness and accidents in aviation discourse. *Language in Society*, 17, 357–399.

MACCOBY, N. (1980). Promoting positive health behaviors in adults. In L.A.Bond and J.C.Rosen (Eds) *Competence and Coping during Adulthood*. Hanover, NH: University Press of New England.

MADDUX, J.E. and ROGERS, R.W. (1983). Protection motivation and self-efficacy: a revised theory of fear appeals and attitude change. *Journal of Experimental Social Psychology*, 19, 469–479.

MARSH, P., HARRE, R. and ROSSER, E. (1978). *The Rules of Disorder*. London: Routledge and Kegan Paul.

MILGRAM, S. (1974). *Obedience to Authority.*, New York: Harper and Row.

MILGRAM, S., BICKMAN, L. and BERKOWITZ, O. (1969). Note on the drawing power of crowds of different size. *Journal of Personality and Social Psychology*, 13, 79–82.

MILGRAM, S., and TOCH, H. (1969). Collective behavior: Crowd and social movements. In G. Lindzey and E. Aronson (Eds) *The Handbook of Social Psychology, 2nd edition*. Reading, Mass.: Addison-Wesley.

MORRIS, D. (1981). *The Soccer Tribe*. London: Cape.

MOSCOVICI, S., LAGE, E. and NAFFRECHOUX, M. (1969). Influence of a consistent minority on the responses of a majority in a colour perception task. *Sociometry*, 32, 365–380.

MOSCOVICI, S. and PERSONNAZ, B. (1980). Studies in social influence, V: minority influence and conversion behaviour in a perceptual task. *Journal of Experimental Social Psychology*, 16, 270–282.

MYERS, D.G. (1993). *Social Psychology, 4th edition*. New York: McGraw-Hill.

NEMETH, C., SWEDLUND, M. and KANKI, G. (1974). Patterning of the minority's responses and their influence on the majority. *European Journal of Social Psychology*, 4, 53–64.

NEWCOMB, T.M. (1943). *Personality and Social Change*. New York: Dryden.

PETTY, R.E., WELLS, G.L. and BROCK, T.C. (1976). Distraction can enhance or reduce yielding to propaganda: thought disruption versus effort justification. *Journal of Personality and Social Psychology*, 34, 874–884.

PETTY, R.E and CACIOPPO, J.T. (1986). *Communication and Persuasion: Central and Peripheral Routes to Attitude Change*. New York: Springer-Verlag.

PETTY, R.E., CACIOPPO, J.T., STRATHMAN, A.J. and PRIESTER, J.R. (1994). To think or not to think: exploring two routes to persuasion. in S.Shavitt and T.C.Brock (Eds) *Persuasion*. Boston: Allyn and Bacon.

REICHER, S.D. (1984). The St Pauls' riot: an explanation of the limits of crowd action in terms of a social identity model. *European Journal of Social Psychology*, 14, 1–21.

RENO, R.R., CIALDINI, R.B. and KALLGREN, C.A. (1993). The trans-situational influence of social norms. *Journal of Personality and Social Psychology*, 64, 104–112.

ROBINSON, P. (1978). *Language Management in Education*. Sydney: Allen and Unwin.

ROSENTHAL, R. and DEPAULO, B. (1979). Sex differences in eavesdropping on non-verbal cues. *Journal of Personality and Social Psychology*, 37, 273–85.

SABINI, J. (1995). *Social Psychology, 2nd edition*. New York: Norton.

SCHACHTER, S. (1951). Deviation, rejection and communication. *Journal of Abnormal and Social Psychology*, 46, 190–207.

SCHERER, K.R. (1981). Speech and emotional states. In J.K. Darby (Ed) *Speech Evaluation in Psychiatry*. New York: Grune and Stratton.

SHERIF, M. (1935). A study of some social factors in perception. *Archives of Psychology*, No.187.

SHERIF, M. and SHERIF, C.W. (1969). *Social Psychology*. New York: Harper and Row.

SHERIF, M., HARVEY, O.J., WHITE, B.J., and SHERIF, C. (1961). *Intergroup Conflict and Cooperation: the Robbers Cave Experiment*. Norman, OK: University of Oklahoma Institute of Intergroup Relations.

SLATER, P.E. (1955). Role differentiation in small groups. In A.P. Hare, E.F. Borgatta and R.F. Bales (Eds) *Small Groups*. New York: Knopf.

SMITH, P.B. and BOND, M.H. (1993). *Social Psychology Across Cultures*. New York: Harvester Wheatsheaf.

SNYDER, M. (1979). Self-monitoring processes. *Advances in Experimental Social Psychology*, 12, 85–128.

SNYDER, C.R. and FROMKIN, H.L. (1980). *Uniqueness: the Human Pursuit of Differences*. New York: Plenum.

STEIN, R.T., HOFFMAN, L.R., COOLEY, S.J., and PEARCE, R.W. (1980). Leadership valence: modelling and measuring the process of emergent leadership. In J.G. Hunt, and L.L. Larson (Eds) *Crosscurrents in Leadership*. Carbondale, Ill.: Southern Illinois University Press.

STRODTBECK, F.L., JAMES, R.M. and HAWKINS, C. (1958). Social status in jury deliberations. In E.E. Maccoby, T.M. Newcomb, and E.L. Hartley (Eds), *Readings in Social Psychology, 3rd edition*. New York: Holt.

TURNER, R.H. (1974). Collective behaviour. In R.E.L. Faris (Ed.) *Handbook of Modern Sociology*. Chicago: Rand McNally.

TURNER, V.M. (1967). *The Forest of Symbols*. Ithaca, NY: Cornell University Press.

VAN AVERMAET, E. (1996). Social influence in small groups. In M. Hewstone, W. Stroebe and G.M. Stephenson (Eds) *Introduction to Social Psychology, 2nd edition*. Oxford: Blackwell.

WILDER, D.A. (1986). Social categorization: implications for creation and reduction of intergroup bias. *Advances in Experimental Social Psychology*, 19, 291–355.

WILKE, H. and VAN KNIPPENBERG, A. (1996). Group performance. In M. Hewstone, W. Stroebe and G.M. Stephenson (Eds) *Introduction to Social Psychology, 2nd edition*. Oxford: Blackwell.

FURTHER READING

ARGYLE, M. (1988). *Bodily Communication, 2nd edition*. London: Methuen.. An extensive review of research on non-verbal communication.

ARGYLE, M. (1994). *The Psychology of Interpersonal Behaviour, 5th edition*. London: Penguin. Deals with leadership and other social skills.

BARON, R.A. and BYRNE, D. (1997). *Social Psychology: Understanding Human Interaction, 8th edition*. Boston: Allyn and Bacon. Chapter 4 has an excellent review of the persuasion research.

GILES, H. and COUPLAND, N. (1991). *Language, Contexts and Consequences*. Milton Keynes: Open University Press. A very readable account of the use of language in social situations.

HOGG, M. A. and ABRAMS, D. (1988). *Social Identifications*. London: Routledge. A good account of theories of crowds, especially social identity theory and de-individuation.

MILGRAM, S. and TOCH, H. (1969). Collective behavior: crowds and social movements. In G. Lindzey and E. Aronson (Eds) *The Handbook of Social Psychology, Vol. 4, 2nd edition*. Reading, MA: Addison-Wesley. Contains an extensive review of work on crowds.

SABINI, J. (1995) .*Social Psychology*, 2nd edition. New York: W.W. Norton. Chapter 2 contains an excellent critical account of the research on obedience.

VAN AVERMAET, E. (1995). Social influence in small groups. In M. Hewstone, W. Stroebe and G. M. Stephenson (Eds) *Introduction to Social Psychology: a European Perspective, 2nd edition*. Oxford: Blackwell. An excellent account of the work on conformity and obedience.

WILKE, H. and VAN KNIPPENBERG, A. (1996). Group performance. In M. Hewstone, W. Stroebe and G. M. Stephenson (Eds) *Introduction to Social Psychology, 2nd edition*. Oxford: Blackwell. Includes a good account of the emergence of leaders in groups.

ANSWERS TO SELF-ASSESSMENT QUESTIONS

SAQ 1 An utterance will not influence the listener in the way desired unless words and concepts are used which he or she can understand.

SAQ 2 Politeness is important in order not to damage another's self-esteem. This is done by praising the other person rather than oneself, making indirect requests which give the other choices, and not breaking rules.

SAQ 3 Paying attention to non-verbal cues, especially tone of voice, which is controlled less than facial expression, can help us find out what other people are really feeling.

SAQ 4 People conform to norms in order not to be rejected or laughed at, or because they think the others know best.

SAQ 5 Compliance is conforming in the presence of the group, but not when away from the group, and not believing in the norm. Internalization is when a group member really accepts the norm and conforms to it regardless of whether group members are present.

SAQ 6 In groups which are cohesive, other members are unanimous, the behaviour is publicly visible, and a member is keen to be accepted by the group, or is of low status.

SAQ 7 Culture has the greatest effect – there is more conformity in collectivist cultures. Personality has little effect – though high self-monitors conform more, those who want to be unique less. Gender has almost no effect, if status is held constant.

SAQ 8 When the members of the minority are consistent, with each other and over time, and when they are also flexible and willing to compromise, they are most likely to be able to influence the majority.

SAQ 9 Breaking a rule causes so much trouble because it disrupts behaviour so much – like driving on the wrong side of the road.

SAQ 10 Conditions when people are most likely to be obedient include when given orders by someone in authority, especially if they have power to punish disobedience; when it is believed that they are entitled to give orders, as with doctors; when it is embarrassing to confront the person in authority; and when there is no peer group support.

SAQ 11 The experimenter appeared to be a responsible authority, he used an authoritarian manner which may have elicited unthinking obedience, he did not seem to be worried, and the participants had become gradually committed while giving smaller shocks.

SAQ 12 Only some of them behaved badly, though the others did not stop them. They were playing the role of prison guard as they saw it, and thought they needed to use some degree of coercion for disobedient prisoners. Once the prisoners had been degraded they could be looked on as subhuman.

SAQ 13 A verbal message can influence behaviour or attitudes by showing the recipients the advantage to them of the suggested behaviour, or by the unthinking effects of the attractiveness or status of the source.

SAQ 14 The kinds of messages which are seen as most persuasive are those given by people who are seen as experts; who are attractive; or seen as having high status. People who have verbal and non-verbal skills, like fluency, expressive speech style, and assertive gestures are also more persuasive.

SAQ 15 Those who are most persuadable include the young; the less well-informed; people who have low self-esteem; people who are in a good mood; intelligent people (if the message is complex and well-argued; the less intelligent are influenced more if the argument is weak).

SAQ 16 If you want to influence someone, it is easier to try to do this face-to-face, if you have a good argument and can appeal to a real need of the recipient. Often a large request followed by much smaller one, or a very small request followed by a larger one will be effective.

SAQ 17 Assertiveness is very useful in many work situations, some leisure situations, and with friends. Others can be influenced without upsetting them, and individuals have more control over what happens in a situation.

SAQ 18 The person likely to emerge as leader of a group will have skills or knowledge about what the group is doing. Other, weaker, factors include being male, tall, intelligent, and having certain social skills.

SAQ 19 Emergent leaders were originally members of the group, and have little power to reward or punish. Appointed leaders usually come from outside and have definite powers to reward and punish.

SAQ 20 *Instructing* is needed most when the task is difficult or unclear, *rewardingness* if the group members are having a bad time, and *participation* if the leader is unclear what to do, or suspects that the group may not accept his/her decision.

SAQ 21 Second-line leaders may experience difficulty of communication with those two or more levels below them, since upward communications may be delayed and distorted.

SAQ 22 Le Bon thought that people in crowds are irrational, uncontrolled, and aggressive.

SAQ 23 Freud thought that crowd members form strong ties with each other based on a shared identification with their leader, and that they regress to child-like dependence on him and have no internal restraints.

SAQ 24 De-individuation occurs in larger groups, when people are anonymous, for example in the dark, there is no surveillance of behaviour and no chance of meeting any victims afterwards.

SAQ 25 Social identity theory proposes that self-identity changes to a new identity shared with other crowd members; individuals learn the proper behaviour of members of this group and conform to its norms.

SAQ 26 Religious groups are not aggressive, they are greatly influenced by the leader, and are 'uninhibited' only in special ways prescribed by the group. Football crowds express a lot of aggression, much of it symbolic, and the main focus of interest is opposition to and rivalry with the other group of fans They are very disorderly, though there are shared rituals and costumes.

GLOSSARY

Accommodation: when two interactors shift towards each other's speech style, for example, in accent, speed or loudness.

Accomplice: an assistant of the experimenter, who appears to be another participant, but who has been trained to behave in a particular way, for example, by deviating from a social norm.

After-image: the image which can be seen on a blank wall after looking at a stimulus; it has the complementary colour to the original, for example, yellow-orange in place of blue.

Agentic mode: uncritical obedience to authority, according to Milgram.

Autokinetic effect: when a spot of light is fixated upon and it seems to move.

Back-channel signals: while one person is speaking listeners indicate their reactions by head-nods, short vocalizations and other signals.

Central route: social influence by a communication which the recipient attends to and considers carefully.

Charismatic leader: a leader who can inspire the followers to accept a new vision and pursue new goals.

Cognitive processes: thinking, problem solving, language, memory and so on, which intervene between stimulus and response.

Collectivist cultures: cultures such as in China where great importance is attached to membership of, and harmony in, groups.

Communitas: Victor Turner's term for the state of bonding, love and equality, experienced by young men undergoing initiation rituals.

Compliance: conformity which is only in public, when the group is present, without internalization.

Conformity: the tendency to be affected by others' attitudes, opinions and actions.

Convergence: shifts towards similar behaviour on the part of members of a group or crowd.

Consideration: a leadership style which emphasizes looking after and rewarding the followers.

Crowd: a large number of people gathered together, usually without orderly arrangement.

De-individuation: loss of individual responsibility and restraints by members of some crowds.

Display rules: rules about when emotional expressions, for example, of joy or sadness, should be shown.

Emergent leaders: leaders who emerge in an initially leaderless group, like the foremen of juries.

Ethics committees: committees in departments of psychology which decide whether investigations that might harm participants may be carried out.

First line leaders: leaders who have been appointed to look after a group, for example foremen, sergeants.

Intersubjectivity: taking account of vocabulary and what listeners can be expected to understand when talking to them.

Informational influence: when deviates conform because they take the behaviour of the majority as a source of information, assuming that the others know best.

Initiating structure: a leadership style which emphasizes giving orders and instructions, and organizing work.

Internalization: when a deviate conforms, and really believes in the new norm, for example, conforms when away from the group.

Naïve participants: participants in an investigation who know nothing about its purpose.

Non-verbal communication: communication, especially of emotions and attitudes, to others by facial expression, tone of voice, and other bodily channels.

Norm, social: behaviour or opinions which are shared by members of a group.

Normative influence: conformity through the desire not to be rejected or laughed at.

Performative utterance: utterances like voting or betting which have a direct effect on others, but are not true or false.

Peripheral route: influencing another not by the contents of a communication but by the status or attractiveness of the source or the presentation of the message.

Second-line leaders: leaders like some managers and officers who are directly responsible for first-line leaders, and indirectly for their subordinates.

Self-monitoring: a psychological dimension where those high on it are keen to be accepted and monitor their behaviour in different social situations in order to be accepted.

Self-presentation: behaviour intended to influence the impressions formed by others, for example, by means of clothes and other aspects of appearance.

Social identity: part of the self-image which is based on possessing attributes shared with other members of a group, especially favourable, prestige-giving attributes.

Social rules: behaviour which members of a group agree should be followed, since it prevents serious social problems, as with the rule of the road, or makes new behaviour possible, as with the rules of games.

Socio-emotional leaders: unofficial additional 'leaders' in groups who are concerned about harmony inside the group rather than with the task.

Superego: in Freudian theory, internalized restraints derived from the parents, that is, the conscience.

ACKNOWLEDGEMENTS

Figure 1.1   © Lesley Howling, Barnaby's Picture Library.

Figure 1.2   From Argyle, M., *The Psychology of Interpersonal Behaviour*, 5*th* *edition*. © 1994, Penguin Books, London.

Figure 1.3   From Flanders, N.A. *Analyzing Teaching Behavior*, 1970. Published by Addison Wesley Longman, Inc. © Dr Ned Flanders. Reproduced by kind permission of the author.

Figure 1.4   From Argyle, M., *The Psychology of Interpersonal Behaviour*, 5*th* *edition*. © 1994, Penguin Books, London.

Figure 1.5   Reprinted from *Acta Psychologica*, 28:1, Kendon, A., Some functions of gaze direction in social interaction, pp 1–47, © 1967, with kind permission of Elsevier Science NL, Sara Burgerhartstraat 25, 1055 KV Amsterdam, The Netherlands.

Figure 1.6   From Argyle, M., *Bodily Communication*, © 1975; 1988, Methuen, London.

Figure 2.1   Redrawn by Myers, D.G., *Social Psychology*, 4*th* *edition*, © 1993, McGraw-Hill. Reproduced by kind permission of The McGraw-Hill Companies.

Figure 2.2   From *Psychological Monographs*, 70 (*whole number* 416), Asch, S.E., Studies of independence and conformity: a minority of one against a unanimous majority, © 1956. Reprinted by kind permission of the American Psychological Association.

Figure 2.3   From Myers, D.G. *Social Psychology*, 4*th* *edition*, © 1993, McGraw-Hill. Reproduced by kind permission of The McGraw-Hill Companies.

Figure 2.4   From Myers, D.G. *Social Psychology*, 4*th* *edition*, © 1993, McGraw-Hill. Reproduced by kind permission of The McGraw-Hill Companies.

Figure 2.5   From *Sociometry*, 32, Moscovici, S., Lage, E., and Naffrechoux, M., Influence of a consistent minority on the responses of a majority in a colour perception task, pp 365–380, © 1969.

Figure 3.1   Photograph of Stanley Milgram with the shock generator, reprinted with permission of Alexandra Milgram. Second photograph from the film Obedience, © 1965 Stanley Milgram, and distributed by Penn State Media Sales.

Figure 3.2   From Baron, R. A. and Byrne, D. , *Social Psychology*, 8*th* *edn*. © 1997 by Allyn and Bacon. Reprinted by permission.

Figure 3.3   From *Journal of Personality and Social Psychology*, 34, Petty, R.E., Wells, G.L. and Brock, T.C. Distraction can enhance or reduce yielding to propaganda: thought disruption versus effort justification, © 1976. Reproduced by kind permission of the American Psychological Association.

Figure 3.4   From Myers, D.G., *Social Psychology*, 4*th* *edition*, © 1993, McGraw-Hill. Reproduced by kind permission of The McGraw-Hill Companies.

Figure 3.5   From N. Maccoby (1980), Promoting positive health behaviors in adults. In L. A. Bond and J.C. Rosen (Eds) *Competence and Coping During Adulthood*. Hanover, NH: University Press of New England. Reproduced by kind permission of the Vermont Conferences on the Primary Prevention of Psychopathology.

Figure 3.6   From *Advances in Experimental Social Psychology*, 19, Wilder, D.A., Social categorization: implications for creation and reduction of intergroup bias, pp 291–355, © 1986.

Figure 4.1   © TYT-41-1, Barnaby's Picture Library.

Figure 4.2 (a) and (b)   From *Personnel Psychology*, 15, Fleishman, E.A., and Harris, E.F., Patterns of leadership behavior related to employee grievances and turnover, pp 43–56, © 1962.

Figure 5.1   From Jaffe, Y. and Yinon, Y. Collective aggression: the group-individual paradigm in the study of collective antisocial behaviour. In H.H. Blumberg, A.P. Hare, V. Kent and M.H. Davies (Eds) *Small Groups and Social Interaction*, Vol.1, © 1983 John Wiley and Sons Limited. Reproduced with permission.

Figure 5.2   From Morris, D. *The Soccer Tribe*, 1981, Jonathan Cape Limited. © Eamonn McCabe.

Table 5.1   From Beit-Hallahmi, B. and Argyle, M., *The Psychology of Religious Behaviour, Belief and Experience*. © 1997, Routledge, London.